SALVATION

SALVATION

Jesus's Mission
and Ours

John B. Cobb, Jr.

PROCESS
CENTURY
PRESS

ANOKA, MINNESOTA 2020

Salvation: Jesus's Mission and Ours
© 2020 Process Century Press

Process Century Press
RiverHouse LLC
802 River Lane
Anoka, MN 55303

Process Century Press books are published in association with the International Process Network.

Cover: Susanna Mennicke

VOLUME VI
THEOLOGICAL EXPLORATIONS SERIES
JEANYNE B. SLETTOM, GENERAL EDITOR

ISBN 978-1-940447-46-9
Printed in the United States of America

This series aims to explore the implications of Whiteheadian philosophy and theology for religious belief and practice. It also proposes that process religious thinkers, working from within many different traditions—Buddhist, Confucian, Christian, Hindu, Indigenous, Jewish, Muslim, and others—have unique insights pertinent to the critical issues of our day.

In 1976, we published a book, *Process Theology: An Introductory Exposition,* in which we aimed to "show the creative potentiality of a process perspective in theology." In addition to its explanation of process concepts and their application to Christian doctrine, the book noted the contribution of Whiteheadian thought toward "intercultural and interreligious understanding" and took an early stance on the ecological threat, claiming that process theology was prepared to "make a distinctive contribution" to this challenge.

Since the publication of that book, we have seen many others explore these and other themes in articles, books, and conferences. At the same time, the threat to planetary health and the need for "intercultural and interreligious understanding" has only accelerated. This series is an effort to support theologians and religious philosophers in their ongoing exposition of possible Whiteheadian solutions.

John B. Cobb, Jr.
David Ray Griffin

TABLE OF CONTENTS

PREFACE

I CAN STATE the thesis of this book quite simply. Jesus's mission was to save his people from the Roman yoke. Most of those who shared that mission turned to military means, which Jesus saw to be self-destructive. So, the mission to save his people included saving them from their own proclivity to violence.

Saving his people from Rome and from themselves was the most inclusive mission possible at that time. To follow Jesus today is to adopt the most inclusive mission in our day. That is, to save the world from the self-destruction on which it now seems bent. Some of those who claim to share this goal offer programs that will speed the self-destruction. We need to save the people of the world from themselves as well as from the consequences of our multi-century crimes and mistakes.

Jesus's method is more promising. To me, the call to Jesus's disciples to save the world seems clear and simple. We need to stop serving wealth. We need to love our enemies. But I have not succeeded in making the argument so clear and simple.

Still, I commend the book to the attention of anyone who wants to be a disciple of Jesus. I believe we are called to do our part in "saving the world." If one out of every hundred professed Christians took that call seriously, despite the enormous obstacles, we would have a chance. We could work for that salvation in hundreds of diverse ways, according to our gifts and situations. But if we all recognized the contributions of our brothers and sisters in Christ, and supported one another, the consequences would be even more enormous than the obstacles. Perhaps this book can enable our calling to be a bit more widely heard.

As a nonagenarian, I am constantly asking myself what activities to continue and which to end. I have been attracted to the idea of ending one facet of my career, writing books, with one that put Jesus at the center. I wrote about Jesus's thought of God as Abba. It was a kind of back-to-Jesus appeal that felt OK as a way to conclude my work as a Christian theologian. I think my spiritual life began with a "Papa (Abba) in Heaven" who, like my Papa (and my Mother) on Earth, loved me unconditionally. The difference was that my Papa in Heaven knew me totally and still accepted me. From my parents I could hide quite a lot. Not from God. My theology has not changed much.

Until recently, therefore, I planned no more books. I recognize that some of the work that goes into a good scholarly book is now hard for me, perhaps not even possible. A scholarly book expresses awareness of the literature relevant to the topic, whereas I am far behind on most topics. I can still express myself in lectures and essays of a semi-scholarly form on some topics. I think I have things to say, and I am extraordinarily fortunate to have an audience in China, and now perhaps also in Korea, that has a practical interest in my ideas and proposals. But to organize my ideas, do substantial research, and work the results through a series of drafts is not the way I want to spend what time and energy I still have.

However, I have come to feel that something is missing in my writings. Even though I am not able to write a scholarly book about it, a confessional statement about how I see matters may still be worthwhile. Obviously, a confessional statement will include many opinions that are disputable, and, no doubt, many mistakes. But perhaps there will also be insights of some use to others.

I have written three clusters of books. One is explicitly Christian theology as that is generally understood. A second cluster is on the philosophy of Whitehead and its implications and applications. A third cluster is about the world I hope is coming, what I now call "ecological civilization." In my mind these are all closely related and jointly constitute a coherent theological position. I think it all points to the call to save the world. But I'm not sure that any of my books have made that clear.

The relation of my theology and philosophy was a thematic topic of some of my early books. I adopted Whitehead's philosophy because it seemed to me the best philosophy available. Also, it enabled me to clarify my theological convictions and to relate them critically to the dominant world of thought.

The relation of Whitehead's philosophy to ecological civilization was recognized somewhat vaguely in China, where I did most of my work on ecological civilization. I worked it out most fully in a conference subtitled "Toward an Ecological Civilization" in Claremont in 2015. And in a book that came out of that conference, *Putting Philosophy to Work,* which I coedited with Andrew Schwartz, I made the connection fully explicit.

Most of what I have written on ecological civilization has been published only in Chinese. The Chinese know I am a Christian theologian, and they do not automatically reject my ideas for this reason. They accept those ideas that make sense to them as Marxists, or Confucians, or simply seekers. But writing for this audience does not lead to talk explicitly about theology. Hence the connection of my faith and its theological expression to ecological civilization has remained unformulated. However, it is important to me.

The goal that has dominated my life in recent decades is to move the world toward an "ecological civilization." What I now understand by that term is continuous with what has been my goal ever since, in the late sixties, I was forced to recognize that the fundamental direction of human activities has been toward self-destruction.

I thought then that my task was to call Christians, especially "mainstream" Protestants, to repent of our lack of attention to the nonhuman part of God's creation. I blamed the influence of Immanuel Kant's first two "Critiques" for much of that failure, and I argued that Alfred North Whitehead provided a philosophical alternative that could help Christians recover the more holistic biblical understanding. My contribution was very limited, but the mainline churches did begin to attend to what we called "the ecological crisis."

For a few years, in the early seventies, it seemed possible that, not only the churches, but Western culture generally, would be reshaped by the shared goal of becoming a sustainable society. The United Nations gave excellent leadership. The World Council of Churches added "sustainable" to "just and participatory" in defining the society it sought, and it held conferences all over the world to discuss what this addition meant. Some excellent legislation was passed by the United States Congress and signed into law by Richard Nixon.

In 1973, David Griffin and I organized the Center for Process Studies to ensure that Whiteheadian philosophy would survive to make what contribution it could to the extensive reconstruction that looked possible. We believed that, without an explicit and systematic rejection of the deeper philosophical ideas that have supported the West's unsustainable practices, the effects of these ideas would continue to poison Western practice.

To connect these concerns with Christian theology was all too simple once we freed ourselves from the Kantian dualism. All we had to do was to take seriously the basic Christian teaching of God as Creator. Clearly, Christians should support action to prevent the destruction of much of what is most valuable in God's creation.

Even without the deep philosophical change that process thought offered, the idea of preserving God's creation and generating a sustainable society gave coherence to the goal. There were hundreds of specific tasks to be performed, but they were all part of what Thomas Berry later taught us to call the "great work."

We who felt ourselves part of an indispensable movement did not prepare ourselves well to deal with the opposition we aroused. Those who had a large stake in the unsustainable practices we criticized had enormous power and wealth. They did not attack our positions directly. They never said that sustainability did not matter. But they very quickly, and very skillfully, fragmented what had been, for a few years, a unified movement.

In churches and elsewhere we found lists of important causes replacing the holistic goal of a "sustainable society." We were challenged to prioritize among projects, some of which seemed to require continuing growth of market activity. Tensions between working for the poor and for the natural environment were highlighted. Justice to indigenous people attracted some. Saving the whales from extinction became the focus of concern for others. Some emphasized food production. Others worked for clean air. Etc., etc., etc. Meanwhile, President Bush announced that what needed to be "sustained" was economic growth.

Progress was made on some important fronts. But the economic, political, educational, and social systems remained in place, and despite specific gains, humanity, as a whole, lived more and more unsustainably. While we were concerning ourselves about many worthwhile causes, the neoconservatives were unifying both political parties in support of American imperialism, and the neoliberal economists gained the support of both political parties for an economic system that inevitably concentrates wealth in fewer and fewer hands. Resistance to these developments has been marginal at best.

We have lost forty years to domination by those who are more concerned about the increase of their own wealth and power than the well-being, or even survival, of their fellow humans. There is now no chance of escaping much of the catastrophe that could have been avoided forty years ago, but still, what we do now makes a difference. Perhaps we can still make possible the survival of a significant part of the human population, and also the building of a regenerative society, out of what is left.

We can hardly even begin to develop programs heading in the right direction until we can recover something of the unity we had in the early seventies. We need once again to recognize that many good and important changes are required to achieve a goal in which all of us can believe. If we recognize that we are all partners in seeking a common goal, and we act on this awareness of common interest, however diverse the work that we do, there is a chance of recovering the power to make political and economic changes.

Fortunately, in 2015, Pope Francis offered the world in *Laudato Si* a holistic and unified way ahead. He called it "integral ecology." It recognizes that all parts of the system of life are interdependent with one another and with the inanimate world. Also, humans are an important part of this integrated system. We humans have been disrupting the whole process, but we still have the ability to adopt a constructive role.

Laudato Si deals at once with the problems of the ocean, the land, and the atmosphere, and, also, of human society. Francis's encyclical is at once Roman Catholic teaching, general Christian teaching, and universal human teaching. If humanity would orient its education and research, its economics and its politics, its agriculture and its human culture, by the wisdom of this encyclical, hope for the future could be greatly expanded.

I have been struck not only by the remarkable connection between this pope and Francis of Assissi, but also by the parallels with Jesus of Nazareth. It is widely recognized that Jesus's message was the coming of the *Basileia Theou*, which for reasons explained in this text, I translate as "divine Commonwealth." I believe that Jesus saw what he was proposing, in all its radicality, as the best hope for the salvation of Israel. He believed the Jewish people could avoid destruction by Rome and expulsion from their land precisely by being deeply faithful to their prophetic heritage. He was not successful. Jerusalem was destroyed, and the Jews were expelled from their country.

The pope today is proposing a radically different world from the one we now have. He gives us an account of what would be possible instead of the destruction toward which we are otherwise headed. In short, what he calls "integral ecology" is today's "divine Commonwealth."

We in the Whiteheadian community had been working in this direction since the late sixties, but in a very marginal role. Only in China have we had any historically significant success. This was made possible by the quite independent decision of the Chinese Communist Party to aim for China to become an "ecological civilization." That has given China a goal, comparable to that of Pope Francis and of Jesus, and the process community has the chance to help unpack its meaning and content.

If the papal encyclical was evoking a mass movement and serious study of segments of society where change is most urgent, I would simply encourage everyone to join. Thus far, however, I see more being done under the rubric of "ecological civilization," and since I personally prefer that term, I am continuing with it. It seems an eminently appropriate goal for a disciple of Jesus. I now connect it with Jesus's own proclamation of the "divine Commonwealth." I hope that significant segments of the church may be stimulated to join with the Chinese in pursuit of ecological civilization.

I believe working for integral ecology or for the coming of ecological civilization is, today, the clearest expression of discipleship to Jesus. However, I have not made this clear in my previous writings. I have some hope that there is a "back to Jesus" movement in the church and even among some who have given up on the church. There may be a chance to strengthen that movement by clarifying the current analogues of Jesus's divine commonwealth. Ecological civilization and integral ecology are as crucial today for all humankind as the divine commonwealth Jesus proclaimed might have been for Jews in his time.

Jesus made clear the radically countercultural nature of the divine commonwealth, and we must make clear the radically counter-cultural character of integral ecology or ecological civilization. We will see that Jesus's teaching of universal love, that is, love that includes the enemy, is required for either.

The book will take the following shape: The inclusive question it asks is how we can be disciples of Jesus in our very different time and place.

Chapter One will show that the salvation sought by Jesus was of the Jewish people. But the destruction of Jerusalem and expulsion of the Jews he hoped to avoid took place.

Chapter Two traces developments after his death. There was no possibility of Jesus's original mission succeeding. However, this mission had brought into being communities that lived by his teaching. His disciples reformulated his mission so as to open these communities fully to Gentiles. The church was born, and its mission has focused on small groups (congregations) and salvation of individuals.

Chapters Three and Four treat historical consciousness, which played a large role in the Abrahamic traditions and continued to be part of secular Western thinking until recently. Now its existence cannot be taken for granted. Yet it is only through historical consciousness that we can understand what it means today to be disciples of Jesus.

Jesus saw that Israel was plunging toward self-destruction. We see that this is true of the human species today. Jesus proclaimed the possibility of forming a countercultural society that would offer a way of survival. We can find much in the norms he offered for that society that are applicable in our time. Chapter Five concludes that today's disciple will work for ecological civilization.

Chapters Six, Seven, and Eight explain what an ecological civilization would be like, and Chapter Nine shows how it might be possible for the United States to move some distance in that direction.

Chapters Ten and Eleven probe into the deeper obstacles to any such achievement; not to declare it impossible, but to show how very basic are the required changes in habits of thought and behavior.

Chapter Twelve strikes a more positive note, showing that many developments in the past century have paved the way for the practical adoption of some of the approaches Jesus advocated.

As Christians, we are likely to pray to God for help in this difficult project. Often this seems *pro forma*. Part of the problem is that we have not thought through the sort of help that God gives in distinction from the types of help that we can receive only from other people. Chapter Thirteen concludes the book on this note, hoping that we will look to God for what only Jesus's Abba can do for us.

1

JESUS'S UNDERSTANDING
OF "SALVATION"

"Soteriology," that is, the doctrine of salvation, is a central part of Christian theology. When I joined the church, I professed my faith in Jesus as "Lord and Savior." If one is interested, as I am, in Jesus's understanding of salvation, the most promising place to look is in the sayings attributed to him in the synoptic gospels. But one finds very little talk of "salvation" there.

One phrase attributed to Jesus by both Matthew and Mark is: "He who endures to the end will be saved." Jesus is describing a time of tribulations, and the apparent meaning of being "saved" is to survive. In describing the tribulation, Matthew attributes to Jesus the statement that if God had not shortened the duration, "no flesh would be saved." Again, the meaning is survival. In the synoptic gospels, when people ask Jesus to save them, this is usually the meaning.

There are a few uses that differ from this. In a discussion of who can enter the *basileia theou* (usually translated "Kingdom of God"), Jesus states that it is almost impossible for a rich man to do so. The disciples then ask: Who can be "saved." The meaning of "saved" here is clearly the same as entering the *basileia*. In Luke's account of Jesus dining with the tax-collector, Zacchaeus, when Zacchaeus vows to restore all he has taken unjustly, Jesus says: "Today salvation has come to this house." Clearly the meaning is not very different from the statement that Zacchaeus now lives in the *basileia theou*.

This quick survey of what data we have on Jesus's use of the terms "save" and "salvation" indicates that what he means by these words often has little connection with later soteriology. Sometimes "salvation" is keeping people alive. Sometimes it means their entry into the *basileia theou*.

This book is about Jesus's understanding of salvation and how that directs us as his disciples. What is important for me at the outset is to help the reader avoid reading into Jesus's message ideas that developed later. To put my cards fully on the table, I name two such ideas: one is individualist, and one is cosmic.

Certainly, individuals and their "salvation" play a large role in the synoptic gospels, even when the word is not used. Many individuals are healed, and healing and "salvation" are closely related. This saving can be moral or psychological, as well as physical. A few are even brought back to life. Also, in some instances, as part of the healing process of individuals, Jesus forgives sins.

That many early Christians felt that Jesus's sacrifice of his life had opened the door into a community where they experienced forgiveness is clear. It is also clear that in the early church, services of communion were connected in the minds of congregants with the forgiveness of sins. Mark and Luke support this connection by placing on Jesus's lips at the last supper the teaching that he gave his life for the sake of many. Matthew takes the next, the fateful, step by adding to Jesus's statement "for the forgiveness of sins." He then introduces this idea into the dream in which Joseph is encouraged to marry Mary and play the father role for Jesus. The angel tells Joseph that Mary's son "will save his people from their sins."

In itself, this is harmless. Because of Jesus there were communities of believers whose members experienced, despite their sins, full and loving acceptance by God and by fellow believers. This could have been part of a rich experience of new life without doing theological harm. But, in fact, it became the dominant understanding of Jesus's mission and the center of the doctrine of "salvation." We have seen that this process begins even within the gospels. Matthew's teaching that Jesus gave his life so that we could be forgiven certainly paves the way for later "satisfaction" theories of atonement.

The ransom theory gains explicit support in one saying attributed to Jesus by both Mark and Matthew. "The Son of Man came not to be served but to serve, and to give his life a ransom for many." Jesus may well have said he died for the sake of many. I doubt that he described this in terms of paying a "ransom." Perhaps some Gentile Christians thought of themselves as in bondage to evil powers until they encountered Jesus and joined a community of believers.

The idea of a judgment after death serves as the setting or background for some of Jesus's parables. He uses it to teach that what we do to the humblest of people we are doing also to him. Unfortunately, this background became central to later Christian understandings of salvation. Judgement became focused on each individual for personal sins. Unless these sins are forgiven, it came to be thought, people are destined for everlasting punishment. The church increased its worldly power by claiming to be the mediator of this forgiveness. This understanding of salvation is far removed from Jesus.

The cosmic view is also far removed from Jesus. However, we must acknowledge that messianic expectations of this kind were present in the early church. In the gospel of Mark, some of this is interpolated into Jesus's prediction of the destruction of Jerusalem. "The sun will be darkened, and the moon will not give its light, and the stars will be falling from heaven" (Mark 13:24). Those who want to emphasize the supernatural character of Jesus can appeal not only to this "little apocalypse" in Mark, but also to the imagery in the book of Revelation. Supernaturalist cosmic views have not been nearly as important in the life of the Christian church as the individualist view described above. On the other hand, today the human story is sometimes very helpfully included in a cosmic story, as has been done by Bryan Swimme and Thomas Berry. Sadly, the supernaturalist version is still sometimes read into Jesus's understanding of salvation.

I have entitled this chapter "Jesus's Understanding of Salvation." I want theologically to think about what it means for us now to work for salvation as disciples of Jesus. Nevertheless, in the rest of this chapter, that word will play a secondary role. We assume that Jesus understood his role as bringing what we would call "salvation." We assume that we are also called to take part in salvific work. But this is not the language in which Jesus presented his ideas, and there is no reason for us to limit ourselves to any one terminology.

According to all three synoptic gospels, Jesus's message of salvation was about the *basileia theou*. For Jesus, the good news was that the *basileia theou* was at hand. So, the question about how Jesus understood "salvation" is more usefully formulated as: "What did he mean by the *basileia theou*? What content did that phrase have for him? Yes, it included personal transformation and healing and forgiveness. But these were aspects of something more inclusive.

Jesus told many parables about the *basileia theou*, making it clear that this is extremely important. It is worth giving up everything else to obtain. However, parables that are explicitly about the *basileia theou* generally help rather little in explaining what it is like.

Perhaps the clearest basis for reconstructing what Jesus meant by *basileia theou* is found in his response to the disciples when they asked him to teach them how to pray. His answer was what we call the "Lord's Prayer." It centers on the *basileia theou*. When people bring an individualist understanding of salvation with them, they find meanings in the prayer that may not be part of Jesus's intention. Let's let the prayer tell us what Jesus actually taught. Matthew offers his account in 6:9–13. Below is the Revised Standard Version.

> Our *Abba* who art in heaven, hallowed be thy name.
> Thy *basileia* come,
> Thy will be done on earth as it is in heaven.
> Give us this day our daily bread;
> And forgive us our debts, as we have forgiven our debtors;
> And lead us not into temptation, but deliver us from evil.

It is significant that we address God as our parent rather than as "Lord" or "King." Further, the Aramaic word used by Jesus is "Abba," the language of the infant. It would more accurately be translated "Papa." Instead, I will simply use the word Jesus used.

The prayer is emphatically not about one's personal needs. One does not pray to one's personal Abba. One does not pray for one's individual food or forgiveness. *We* pray to *our* Abba, and *we* ask for *our* bread and *our* forgiveness. We might think that "we" are only believers, but the prayer is about global transformation. We address the Abba of all.

The first petition is that Abba's name be hallowed. Without reverence for Abba, Jesus could not hope for anything. As soon as that is acknowledged, the prayer turns to its fundamental petition, that Abba's *basileia* come. After that we read: "Thy will be done on earth as it is in heaven." In Hebrew writing, often a point is stated a second time in different terms. We may take that to be the case here. The coming of the "*basileia*" would be the arrival of a situation in which Abba's will would be done on earth as it is in heaven. Presuming that Jesus thought Abba's will was completely done "in heaven," the implication is that the *basileia* comes when and where Abba's will *is* done on earth.

The next two petitions identify what Abba wills for the earth. The first is, literally, for bread. We assume it represents food in general. Where rice is the staple, it would do just as well. The prayer is that we have the food we need. I suggest that "bread" represents all that is essential for our livelihood. When God's will is done, the basic physical needs of everyone will be met.

We often pray this prayer as if Jesus were instructing us to pray, in particular, for *our* personal needs, those of the people engaged in praying right then, to be met. But that focus cannot be applied to the previous petition for God's will to be done on earth. Following that petition, this one must be not just for those who are uttering the words, but for all people. The coming of the *basileia* is the end of global hunger. I take it that this represents the end of desperate poverty. When God's will is done, everyone will have enough.

Jesus's vision may have been still more radical. He speaks of "daily" bread being provided "this" day. There is resonance to God's provision of manna for the Israelites as they fled from Egypt. There is explicit prohibition of collecting each day more than is needed for that day. Perhaps we are praying for a world in which all needs are met without hoarding or accumulation. We may think of gathering and hunting societies in which the food for the day is acquired on the day. There is no private wealth.

The second petition that gives content to the *basileia* is about forgiveness. When we ask forgiveness of God, we are thinking of our failure to do all that we ought to do, all that we owe to God. This can be identified either as "sins" or as "debts." It is, of course, possible that Jesus meant for us to think of our relations with one another in the same way. That is, we should forgive all who have sinned against us. This would include their failure to pay what they owe us monetarily.

I do not doubt that, when Jesus called on people to love each other, this included the spirit of forgiveness of the injuries we inflict on one another. But I also believe that the language of *basileia theou* points us toward a changed society. The clearest vision of a changed society in Israel was in the book of Leviticus, in the call for Jubilee. The heart of Jubilee is the forgiveness of monetary debts. Jesus's parables often refer to the forgiveness of monetary debts. That Jesus understood the *basileia theou* to fulfill the hope for Jubilee seems to me eminently plausible, even probable.

In the Jubilee tradition, "debt" may have had a metaphorical use, but it also had quite literal meaning. The book of Leviticus develops the idea of the forgiveness of all monetary debts every fifty years, and Jesus incorporated the Jubilee into his concept of the *basileia theou*. The most often prayed Christian prayer calls, in its origin, for a radical change in the economic order.

One might wonder why Jesus focused on the economic system. This was not strange to the prophetic tradition. The Hebrews, like many Near Eastern peoples, looked back to a time when there was relative equality among people. The main factor that disrupted this equality was debt. However, many of us have thought the practice of forgiving debts periodically would make it impossible to borrow money. Economist Michael Hudson has persuaded me that the debts that were forgiven were usually a failure to pay money owed to the king. When crops failed, the farmer was not able to pay the taxes and fees. This debt grew because even the interest could hardly be paid. Eventually, the farmer lost his farm and even his own freedom. Forgiving this debt did not cheat private lenders out of legitimate repayment.

Not infrequently, it is now thought, a new king forgave the debts of the people to his predecessor. That included liberating those who had become slaves and returning land to those who had been dispossessed. This made the king popular with his people and also restored the health of the society. A society of slaves or landless peasants was not as strong a basis for political and military power as a society of free men with an economic stake in the country.

The Jubilee passage in Leviticus codifies this tradition. We do

not know how often there were actual Jubilees in Israel, but we
know that the ideal was widely appreciated. The Jews knew that
unpayable debts concentrated wealth in fewer and fewer hands.
It was true in the ancient Near East. It is just as true today. Jesus
wanted not only to abolish extreme poverty, but also to end the
system that created it.

For Jesus, our hope for God's forgiveness of us is closely bound
up with our forgiveness of one another. Here, and in other passages,
Jesus is especially harsh toward those who seek forgiveness of their
own debts but fail to forgive others. God cannot forgive the debts
of those who are themselves unforgiving. Apart from our forgiving
of debts to one another, God's will cannot be done on earth.

We cannot spell out how Jesus would, today, develop the
economy of the new society for which he taught us to pray. But it
is unlikely that it would be in the form of unadulterated capitalism.
My main point is only that the Lord's Prayer is about the coming
of an economy radically different from that of Jesus's time and,
perhaps, even more different from the one that dominates today.

Given this interpretation of the prayer, the final petition, as
translated in the Revised Standard Version, seems oddly out of
place. Temptations, as we think of them, are highly individual. I am
glad to say that the translation of this verse also is contested. Some
scholars show that, more literally, it is asking God to preserve us
through the time of troubles. This would be deeply meaningful to
those who thought that the messianic age could come only through
a period of chaos and suffering. That Jesus closed the prayer by
asking for God's help, especially through that period, makes sense.
We, too, have every reason to pray for help in a "time of troubles."

In many of our churches we add another line. This addition
says much more about what later became standard Christian
thinking than about Jesus. "For thine is the power, the kingdom,
and the glory." This would be suitable if the prayer were addressed
to a heavenly king. But it is inappropriate to the worship of Abba.

Sadly, the church was not satisfied to think of God's power on the model of the infant's "Papa." God must be the cosmic ruler. The idea that God is "almighty" and all-controlling replaced the idea of God as all-loving Papa, established itself, and poisoned Christian theology.

It may now be clear why I avoid the common translation of *basileia theou* as "Kingdom of God." When we ask God that "his" *basileia* come we are asking that God reign on earth. I believe Jesus was asking that Israel, in particular, become the locus of God's reign. Since the term *basileia* connotes a reign, the common translation as "kingdom" is entirely understandable. Nevertheless, I consider it misleading because, as we have noted, Jesus shifts from the widespread thinking of God as a uniquely powerful monarch to understanding God as "abba. The *basileia* is where Papa reigns. Papa reigns for the sake of the children, not to lord it over them.

A more appropriate term for the political status produced by the reign of Papa and described by Jesus is "commonwealth." This term suggests that governance is for the sake of the common good of the inhabitants, rather than for the one who rules. It cuts against hierarchical thinking.

We could then speak of the "Commonwealth of God." *Theou* can certainly be translated in that way. But Papa is present in this commonwealth, not as its owner, but in and through the love of each for all. I find this better expressed by calling this common-wealth "divine." Hence, from here on, instead of repeating the Greek words, *basileia theou,* I will speak of the "divine common-wealth." Although what Jesus's followers were to work and pray for was a vast historical change in Israel, the divine commonwealth was already present in communities governed by mutual love. In such communities the basic needs of all were met, and finance was subordinated to human relationships.

There are other important things to be said about the divine commonwealth. One is that it profoundly reverses the dominant cultural values. In the beatitudes we learn that just those whom we are likely to pity—the poor, the meek, the persecuted—are the ones who are truly blessed. Furthermore, this is not only a reversal of evaluations. In the Magnificat, the poem Luke puts on the lips of Mary when she learns that she is to bear a holy child, this reversal is clearly located in history. God "has shown strength with his arm, he has scattered the proud in the imagination of their hearts, he has put down the mighty from their thrones, and exalted those of low degree; he has filled the hungry with good things, and the rich he has sent empty away" (Luke 1: 56-55).

In terms of what we have noted thus far, we might consider that all this reflects rather idle, generalized imagining. When today, we middle-class believers pray before our abundant meals that no one go hungry, it often has that character. However, to read this back into the gospel accounts of Jesus would be a mistake. Jesus is reported in both Matthew and Mark as asserting that the divine commonwealth is "at hand." This indicates that he was not talking about a vision of something that might happen someday. It was happening then, or it was on the verge of happening.

In the story of the rich young ruler, the youth feels that he has followed the law faithfully, but he still lacks something. Jesus tells him that if he wants to be fully whole, he should give his wealth to the poor and become a member of the community that travelled with Jesus. This becoming "perfect" was a possibility "at hand." The young man found the cost too high. But the exchange shows that Jesus thought individuals could enter the divine commonwealth here and now. Elsewhere, also, he asserts that the commonwealth is found in the table fellowship among his disciples. Of course, this does not mean that what we are taught to pray for has already happened. The apostles were taught to pray for a transformation of the nation. We are called to pray for the transformation of the world.

Jesus's fundamental task was to proclaim the divine commonwealth. That his disciples should pray for this is not problematic.

Of course, for Jesus, one does not exhaust one's own responsibility by passing it on to Abba. Jesus gave his life for the realization of the divine commonwealth. He expected his disciples to support him and work for the same end. Praying for success in this mission expressed a strengthening of resolve as much as a petition to God for help.

Jesus thus identified "salvation" with living in community in conformity with God's purposes. In his day, no one thought of a Galilean Jew as bringing salvation to Rome. The messianic hopes were Jewish hopes for Jews. When the Syro-Phoenician woman asked Jesus for help, he initially insisted that his mission was only to Israel. Jesus thought that if Israel would repent, that is, turn its mindset toward conforming to Abba's purposes, the messianic hope would be realized. He found the people of Galilee remarkably receptive. If the temple authorities would lead or join in the crucial reformation, the Jews might have a way of resisting Rome without a self-destructive war.

If we understand that the divine commonwealth is present wherever on earth Abba's will is done, then it is not mysterious that Jesus could point to communities here and there where the divine commonwealth was already present, even though his mission was to actualize it in Israel as a whole. That did not happen. The messianic mission for Israel was not accomplished. But, at least in the circle around Jesus, in their table fellowship, in their care for one another, one could already experience the commonwealth that he hoped for nationally.

The proper response to the nearness of the divine commonwealth was *metanoia*. What, then, is *metanoia?* Literally, it means change of mind. The word is used repeatedly in the New Testament. The usual translation, "repentance," though inadequate, can help toward an understanding. It can connote turning oneself and changing direction, and it can thereby convey part of what is implied by *metanoia*. But, too often, repentance is understood as personal regret for one's individual sins and resolve to commit them no more, with some fear of punishment thrown in. This has been substituted for the dynamic and transformational change that *metanoia* identifies.

Accordingly, thoughtful Christians today are seeking other language. They want to express the richness of the word. One formulation by the Greek Orthodox Church in America asserts that *metanoia* denotes a "change of mind, a reorientation, a fundamental transformation of outlook, of man's vision of the world and of himself, and a new way of loving others and God." If a radically different kind of world is now possible and necessary, it can be actualized only by a fundamental reorientation and reinterpretation of everything. Paul's dramatic change of mind on the road to Damascus is an example of the *metanoia* of which he wrote. In Acts, we are told that the "scales fell from his eyes."

We learn what Jesus expected from the change of mind for which he called by reading Matthew's account of the Sermon on the Mount. The demands are radical indeed. Those who have wanted to be Jesus's disciples have generally interpreted them in ways that make them more practical, not dependent on the radical change of orientation for which Jesus called. Indeed, Matthew himself probably toned them down. But Jesus was not telling people how to live in the "real" world of his time. They were called to live in the divine commonwealth, even though it had not yet come into being.

To love not only one's neighbors, but also one's enemies, is a central expression of the needed shift. Jesus pointed out that even Gentiles often loved their neighbors. That is rather natural and easy. But Abba loves everyone unconditionally. Being loved in that way makes it possible for us to love Abba and other human beings in that way. We are called to this. This kind of love characterizes those communities that can be regarded as already embodying the divine commonwealth.

But how did Jesus suppose that unconditional love of all would change the situation of Israel as an exploited Roman province? How did Jesus propose to connect this kind of new spiritual reality with making a difference in relation to Rome? Of course, our knowledge of what Jesus thought is very limited. But we do have a key illustration of how Jesus hoped that change would occur. This is his teaching about going a second mile. This is clearly not a proposal relevant under all circumstances. Jesus was seeking a solution to a specific historical problem. How could love of all people, including Romans, be expressed in such a way as to improve the conditions of the Jewish people?

Rome gave to each of its soldiers the right to force a Jew to carry his gear for a mile. But after the mile is completed, the Jew must be allowed to resume his own business. Jesus proposed that, even though the Jew was free to go, he should instead carry the gear another mile.

How would that change the situation? The relation established during the first mile is that of master and slave. Whereas in much of his life as a soldier, the soldier is himself little better than a slave, here he is the superior, the one with power. This encourages an attitude of contempt toward the one he is forcing to work for him. On the part of the Jew, this forced labor and the soldier's contempt intensify resentment and the desire for revenge.

But what happens in the second mile? The soldier will be taken aback. This worthless scum turns out to be a voluntary helper. He is a human being, and a quite remarkable one at that. He deserves to be treated as such. The exploited Jew is no longer acting under compulsion. He is acting as a free man. As a free man he embodies God's love, even for this heretofore cruel soldier. He sees the confusion, and perhaps some sign of gratitude, on the part of the soldier. At least to some extent, the master/slave relation morphs into a companionship. These soldiers are forced to live as servants of officers who typically make harsh demands and are little concerned about their well-being. It is not too hard for Jews to develop some fellow feeling for them. Jesus proposed a practical method for two groups of exploited people to move from enmity to fellow feeling.

But what about their officers? Could Jewish peasants change the relation with these by showing love? I do not know of explicit teachings of Jesus. But we do have stories of action. A centurion asked Jesus for help in saving the life of his daughter. Jesus responded in love. How, then, could the centurion continue to think of these Galileans contemptuously? More reciprocal relations might become possible.

Roman oppression was felt by Jews most directly through the military. But equally important was taxation. Rome used indigenous people as collectors of the taxes. Some Jews would take this job, with its onus and virtual exclusion from the Jewish community, because Rome's might would support them in collecting more than what was needed to pay taxes to Rome. They could enrich themselves. The other Jews were thus doubly oppressed by the system.

We have referred earlier to a tax collector named Zacchaeus. Jesus sees that this man is interested in him and visits Zacchaeus's home. We do not know what went on between them. But Zacchaeus vows to reverse his exploitative actions. Jesus may have thought that if the larger Jewish community dealt more compassionately with those who collected Rome's taxes, the tax collectors would do their work less exploitatively.

In short, Jesus may well have believed that if Roman foot-soldiers, Roman officers, and those Jews who collected Roman taxes were all treated in love by the Jewish community, the Roman Empire would not be experienced as so oppressive. Roman rule was not purely evil. Rome offered some benefits in exchange for its exploitation. A friendly relation between Jewish peasants and the representatives of Roman rule would accent the positive and minimize the negative aspects of being part of the empire.

The response of Galilean peasants was promising for Jesus's third way. But the salvation of Israel required the support of the temple establishment, as well. Jesus journeyed to Jerusalem, knowing full well the dangers. He believed that the temple authorities were using their prerogatives for themselves rather than for the spiritual good of Israel. Many peasants felt exploited by them. Jesus said that they had made of the house of prayer a den of thieves. For the coming of the divine commonwealth, the temple must be purified, and its officials must commit themselves to their sacred calling. On arrival in Jerusalem, Jesus went directly to the temple to begin the process of purification by driving out the money changers. This is the one story we have of Jesus acting violently.

Jesus may have hoped that his act of "cleansing" the temple would evoke repentance from the temple authorities. If so, he was disappointed. On the other hand, there is no indication that they punished him for disturbing the peace. Still, it is reasonable to suppose that they did not appreciate his verbal and physical attack. Our gospel accounts of Jesus's last days suggest that they led in his arrest and trial. Thus, they play the villain's role in the gospels.

Scholars have pointed out that the telling of the story to Gentiles would tend to exaggerate the Jewish role in comparison with that of the Romans. Even the gospels make clear that it was Rome that crucified him as one who claimed kingship of the Jews. Rather than present their new lord as an enemy of Rome, Gentile believers might prefer to present him as a Jewish critic of the Jewish priesthood. Some speculation about what happened from the perspective of the Jewish leaders may help to balance accounts.

Rome was unusually harsh toward Jews because Jews were unusually resistant to its rule. Matters had come to a head over worship of the emperor. For Romans, it made sense that people worship power. The one in power then gains in strength through their worship. Worship of the emperor helped to hold the empire together. Such worship should take place in the temple. But the Jewish response to such a sacrilege was violent.

Rome dealt harshly with rebels but negotiated with Jewish leaders. These leaders persuaded the Romans to excuse Jews from formal worship as long as they expressed their allegiance in other ways. This made it possible for the Jewish people to survive both in Palestine and throughout the empire. In later years, Jesus's Gentile followers would try to take advantage of this Jewish privilege with some success. Meanwhile, confronted by Jesus's call for a third way, the Jewish leaders may well have felt that this is what they had already achieved.

In any case, the temple authorities rejected Jesus's call to "repent, for the divine commonwealth is at hand." Jesus's crucifixion ended the promising beginnings in Galilee. Zealots continued to stir up opposition to Rome. The Jews revolted twice. Rome destroyed Jerusalem and expelled the Jews from Israel.

2

"SALVATION" IN CHRISTIAN HISTORY

Probably little would have come of Jesus's abortive mission if his intention to transform Israel had not been enlarged. Our gospel writers were fully aware of this move. The prayer Jesus taught his disciples at least leaves open how widely God's purposes might be actualized on earth. The gospels (especially Luke) tell us how frequently Jesus found a response outside the Jewish community. His parables and teachings emphasized that others could respond to God and benefit from their relations with God. In the book of Acts, Luke continues this story of including Gentiles. Paul plays the largest role.

Luke recognizes that the *basileia theou* was Jesus's goal, and that this was meaningful only for Jews. In his gospel this leads to the emphasis, noted above, that although Jesus's central message was about Jews and was addressed to Jews, even during his ministry, he attended to the needs of others. But Luke still wanted to explain the great change in mission that occurred after Jesus's crucifixion.

To establish some continuity between Jesus's own mission to Israel and the great attraction of Jesus to Gentiles, Luke opens his second book, "The Acts of the Apostles," by dealing with this question explicitly. Acts begins with the final conversation between the resurrected Jesus and his disciples. They ask whether now, in his resurrected form, Jesus will "restore the *basileia* to Israel." Even though Luke, in his gospel, moves the message of the divine commonwealth away from any supernatural understanding, in Acts we get the suggestion that, at least after the resurrection, this form of the expectation reappears. It sounds as though the inquiry is about a supernatural imposition of the divine commonwealth.

I wish that Luke reported Jesus as explicitly rejecting that form of hope, but, regrettably, he leaves the door open. In Luke's account, Jesus only rejects the idea that proclaiming the divine commonwealth as *at hand* is now meaningful. When it comes, and how, are no longer the concern of Jesus's disciples. In later times, many would walk through the door Luke leaves ajar.

In any case, Luke makes clear that the disciples of Jesus now have a different task. The new reality is the coming of the Holy Spirit. The words Luke puts on Jesus's lips are: "It is not for you to know times or seasons which your Father has fixed by his own authority. But you shall receive power when the Holy Spirit has come upon you, and you shall be my witnesses in Jerusalem, and in all Judea and Samaria and to the end of the earth" (Acts 1:7–8).

Clearly, the message now is not about the divine commonwealth as a way of saving Israel from destruction. Although Jesus failed in his effort to save Israel, the resurrected Jesus wants the disciples to witness to him. This is a dramatic change, but there is a connection between Jesus's proclamation of political salvation in the coming of the divine commonwealth and the new experience of the Holy Spirit. The coming of the commonwealth involved vast numbers of people adopting a new lifestyle and the emergence of communities of such people. In much smaller numbers, this had happened. And for them, Jesus's resurrection meant that even in his failure to save Israel as a whole, he had been the anticipated

Messiah. The Greek word for the Messiah is Christ. For the new communities of disciples of Jesus, Jesus was the Christ. These communities, and the church into which they developed, embodied the achievements of Christ in all their ambiguity.

We would judge that the spirit in the new communities, even before Pentecost, was already a very holy spirit. However, Luke sees that, after Jesus's death and resurrection appearances, the communities of disciples received the Holy Spirit in a new way, a way that empowered all who believed. This prepares us to understand the extraordinary work of Paul, who saw that, by the power of the Holy Spirit, all were freed from the law, especially the requirement of circumcision. These new communities were equally open to Jews and Gentiles, males and females, slaves and their masters. This certainly had political significance, but the focus is on the personal and the social.

We saw that Luke softened the dramatic difference between the time of Jesus's ministry and the testimony to him after his resurrection by accenting how, already in his ministry, what was happening among his followers was like what happened in the early congregations. Similarly, through all the subsequent changes, we can trace some continuity between what happened in these congregations and what happened in the later churches. Nevertheless, there have been repeated changes, many of which have created disturbing rifts.

Rita Nakashima Brock and Rebecca Parker wrote a book entitled *Saving Paradise: How Christianity Traded Love of This World for Crucifixion and Empire.* Studying ancient church buildings, they found that these were typically decorated with scenes of paradise. Jesus was depicted as teacher and shepherd. They decided that for centuries Christians found that their life together was a foretaste of paradise.

The expectation of historical change for which Jesus worked was replaced in the Gentile world by the experience of a new life in a community of love and mutual support, undergirded by expectation of paradise after death. Probably most of the Gentile converts had little understanding of the Jewish expectation of a Messiah, the expectation that shaped Jesus's thinking about salvation. For the Gentiles, the assurance of a blessed hereafter, continuing the joy they experienced in countercultural communities of mutual love, enabled them to appropriate much of Jesus's teaching.

On one occasion (I Corinthians 15:19), Paul stated that if there were no resurrection of the dead, believers were the most pitiable of all men. Clearly, he did not think that physical death was the end. He called believers to participate in the suffering and death of Jesus, with the assurance that they would then also participate in his resurrection.

Nevertheless, when we compare Paul's writings to later Christian ones, we find there is far less focus on what happens after death. In Paul's congregations, there was a strong sense of the presence of a truly holy Spirit. How this was related to the risen Christ and to Abba (Jesus's God) was not entirely clear or particularly important. Paul assumed that this presence was a reality that death would not end. Hence, even though later generations of Christians focused more attention on questions of after life than Paul, and less on participation here and now in the Spirit, they did not feel any sharp break with him.

We often speak of the "fall" of the church, that is, of its loss of any real conformation to Jesus's teaching, as coming with its establishment by Constantine. His interest in the church was at least partly political, and to serve his purposes it needed to agree on doctrine. Those who would not agree to the Nicene Creed were banished. To some extent, correct doctrine became more important than faith or faithfulness. And, certainly, when established, purified of theological dissent, the "orthodox" church was no longer purified by occasional persecution. It was no longer countercultural. One suspects that when joining the church was no longer dangerous, and began, instead, to contribute to one's power and wealth, the congregations developed characteristics that did not fit with the paradise idea. The church even persecuted others.

Nevertheless, it seems that, for many Christians, the church remained a very positive part of their lives. As the empire crumbled, the importance of the church for dealing with personal and social crises increased. For many people, the idea that it was a sanctuary from the chaos of the decaying state was probably quite meaningful. Some sense of its being a foretaste of paradise was still credible.

Brock and Parker see the greatest corruption as coming with Charlemagne. He used the church in his efforts to subjugate the Saxons. The Saxons were Christians, but they had a theology he could accuse of heresy. He got his preachers to tell his soldiers that God would reward them for killing the Saxon heretics. The path was paved to the Crusades. Again, and again, Christians would be assured by their leaders that killing Muslims would please their God. Christian churches became recruitment centers for killing the supposed enemies of Christ.

What was communicated in this new theology was what I call Christianism. Supporting the political and even military strength of the institution replaced serving humanity as discipleship to Jesus. Saint Francis showed what discipleship to Jesus truly meant, and his popularity showed that the gospel could still play a role in Christendom. But it no longer was central to the official teaching of the churches. In some, being Christian was doing the things that would gain God's approval and get you into heaven. This shift was accompanied by an increased emphasis on the horrors of hell. The church morphed into an institution that could assist people in going to heaven rather than to hell.

The forgiveness of sins had always been an important part of Christianity. But this had followed from the assurance that God loved us and expressed that love by sending Jesus to witness to it, even giving his life. The people who gathered and experienced a foretaste of paradise loved each other in a way that meant they forgave one another unconditionally, as God forgave them. Now the forgiveness of one's sins became the only way to avoid eternity in hell, and the doctrine of God's loving character faded behind the church's control over God's forgiveness.

Jesus had shown the meaning of loving even one's enemies when, on the cross, he forgave those who crucified him. Now the cross took on a new importance. The tortured Saxons identified with the tortured Jesus. Western Christian art began to feature the suffering of Jesus on the cross, with which suffering Christians identified. Jesus's sacrifice of his life came to be seen as, in itself, a salvific act. In this new context, in which security from being punished for one's sins was central, Jesus's death was thought to have played a role in gaining our forgiveness by God. The doctrine of atonement became central to theology. Our sin called for punishment, but God caused Jesus to suffer in our stead. The heaven that Jesus makes possible for us became discontinuous with anything believers experienced in the church.

It was understood that the appropriation of the benefits of Jesus's death required "faith." Although this "faith" was not supposed to be simply a matter of intellectual belief, being an orthodox believer and obedient to the commands of the church became very closely associated with gaining God's forgiveness in exchange for Jesus's suffering.

My formulation expresses my deep regret that so much of Christianity morphed into this quite different religion. Even so, it would be wrong to imply that this new theology of Jesus's atonement for our sins has no basis in Jesus's teaching. Overcoming the power of sin was certainly important to Jesus.

Jesus's central proclamation was a call for repentance in view of the coming of the divine commonwealth. To repent implies that there is something wrong with the given state of affairs, something of which people should repent. Some interpreted what was wrong as individual "sin;" so the forgiveness of sin would be central to salvation. However, as noted in the previous chapter, the Greek word we translate as "repent" is *"metanoia,"* which identifies simply a change of mind. For the Greeks, thinking wrong was not necessarily a matter of sin. For Jesus, the wrongness of the dominant pattern of thinking certainly led to much sin in Israel, but the primary need was not being forgiven. Instead, it was to adopt Jesus's understanding of the divine commonwealth and to reorient the whole of life accordingly. Reducing this to the problem of personal guilt missed the point.

I believe that we have all sinned and that we all need forgiveness. I believe that the mutual love into which we are called involves mutual forgiveness. I believe there is much for which we need God's forgiveness. I believe that recognizing that we are sinners in need of forgiveness can often lead toward authentic faith. I do not want to attack the view that there is a close connection between salvation and the forgiveness of sins.

However, I do want to oppose the idea that emphasizing our sinfulness and the great lengths to which God has gone to forgive us has any basis in Jesus's own teaching. Jesus believed that there is a better way, a much better way, to organize our lives together. Forgiving and being forgiven are important contributions as inherent in mutual, unconditional love. Abstracted from that context they do not constitute the divine commonwealth.

For some forms of Christian evangelism, the first step is to heighten and make fully conscious feelings of guilt and, sometimes, fear of punishment after death. The idea is that until one fully recognizes one's need for forgiveness, the assurance of that forgiveness will not mean much. If forgiveness is equivalent to salvation, then one's awareness of sin becomes central. In a sense, the guiltier one feels the better.

Shifting the church's understanding of salvation to a focus on Jesus's suffering so that God would, or could, forgive us was the capstone of this catastrophic development. It supported the Christianism that replaced discipleship. It turned Christianity into a religion that has been increasingly felt as incredible in the modern world. And, if one did believe it, it would do more harm than good. Fortunately, the teaching of the church has never been reduced to this formula, but for many Christians, salvation is understood as God's forgiveness of our sins, which is made possible by Jesus's sacrificial death. This forgiveness will prevent the eternal punishment that might otherwise be our destiny.

Sadly, the sins that have usually been highlighted in order to generate guilt have not been those that are central to Jesus. For Jesus, our basic, comprehensive sin is our failure to love God and our neighbors as ourselves. If we called attention to the importance of this love, and offered help in its growth and increased role in the lives of believers, the centrality of guilt might not be destructive.

What has been profoundly destructive is that Christian legalisms have developed that are far worse than the Jewish legalism from which Paul freed the early church. Perhaps the worst features have come from the prominent role of sex that played so small a part in the thought of Jesus and Paul. Once the church had established the idea that sexuality in general was evil, it could persuade almost everyone that they were terribly sinful. Normal and healthy sexual feelings became sins, and normal sexual activities were condemned. So extensive has been this tendency in Christianity that when many people today hear about morality, they expect the topic to be sex.

Sexuality is extremely important. The need for wise guidance both for individuals and for society is great. There has been real progress in recent times. That our sexuality is a gift that can contribute greatly to individual life and to society is widely recognized and appreciated. But the growing tendency to give first place to sexual enjoyment in our quest for human wholeness can also lead to much that is destructive. Regrettably, the churches, for the most part, and for centuries contributed more harm than benefit in this immensely important and immensely difficult area. At last we can celebrate the degree of genuine repentance that is occurring. May it lead to wisdom!

My reason for highlighting and complaining about these historical developments of the Christian understanding of salvation is that I am asking in this book for serious consideration to be given to adopting Jesus's understanding of salvation, even, and, perhaps especially, by some who have rejected what they have taken to be Christianity. Too many Christians assume that the forgiveness of sins, which Jesus certainly affirmed and practiced, must be central to his understanding. Too many Christians have supposed that the sins to be forgiven can be legalistically listed. Too many inhabitants of Christendom have thought that the most important sins are sexual. There is no chance that we will ever become real disciples of Jesus unless we clear our minds of these mistakes.

✴ 3 ✴

CHRISTIANITY AS A
HISTORICAL FAITH

IN CHAPTER ONE I explained my understanding of Jesus's message as profoundly political. His concern could certainly be called "salvation." But the salvation about which he and most Jews of his time cared most deeply was the salvation of Israel. For some Jews, this would have to be a military salvation. For Jesus, it could only be accomplished by a profound political *metanoia*. His crucifixion ended any possibility of success of his mission. To be his disciple could no longer be to proclaim his message of the imminence of the divine commonwealth.

Nevertheless, the resurrected Jesus is reported to have issued, as his last commandment to his followers, that they should make disciples of all people (Matthew 23:19-20). It seems that he wanted us to be disciples. At least we can be sure that his closest followers understood that they were called to convince all who would listen of the good news. What could that mean?

The basic question of this book is: What does that mean for us today? For some of us the answer to that question is life-determining. But serious reflection about it requires asking a prior

37

question. What has it meant for those who sought to be Jesus's disciples over the centuries, beginning with the apostles themselves? When it was clear that Jesus's mission to save Israel had failed and that there was no useful way to pursue it directly, what should the apostles themselves do? What should they call others to do?

In the previous chapter I traced, in broad strokes, the changing meaning that the church gave to discipleship over the centuries. My account makes clear that I think the meaning of discipleship had to be different after the crucifixion than before, and it suggests approval of what discipleship became in the Pauline churches. However, my account also implies that there was much confusion and many mistakes in the later history. Judgments about what discipleship means can be wrong, and wrong judgments can dominate the church. The church, including its understanding of its mission, must change as its historical situation changes. But changes can be so wrong as to turn the church into an enemy of Jesus. Protestants for some time, rightly identifying distortions and corruption in the Catholic church, and overlooking their own distortions and corruptions, identified the popes as "anti-Christ."

We can find similar situations in the Bible. Most of those who want to be disciples of Jesus trace their heritage to the Hebrew prophets, as did Jesus himself. Those prophets often condemned the Hebrew community, and especially its leadership, for radical unfaithfulness.

Whereas for them, as for Jesus, faithfulness to God called for countercultural behavior, the institutions we call "religious" tend to be integrated into the culture. Their beliefs and practices may influence the culture, often for good. But the culture certainly affects them. Jewish culture shaped the synagogue and, among Christians, the dominant Greco-Roman culture shaped the early church.

Our review of what the church has taught at later times was designed to show the radically historical nature of Christianity. It described some forms taken by Christianity that work in ways radically counter to that of Jesus. If we wish to be disciples of Jesus, we certainly cannot take all tradition as normative. Perhaps study of the past can free us from the idea that returning to some period in the past will solve our problems. Like every period in the past, we must find present answers. However, we may find guidance in history to at least avoid some of the worst mistakes.

This whole approach emphasizes that, for Christians, history is constitutive of theology. Jesus understood that he had a role to play that could not have been played anywhere else or, even in Israel, either earlier or later. The role of discipleship necessarily changed with his crucifixion. Later, with the church's establishment, it necessarily changed again. Now that, in the popular mind, Christianity is so often identified with Christianism, and Christianism is rightly rejected, the task of the disciple will certainly be different. And I propose that the self-destruction in which the modern world is engaged once again calls for a reformulation of Christian mission.

There is a sense in which every community, every tradition, every system of belief is historical. But that is not the way that all traditions understand themselves. History is not constitutive of all. Indeed, it seems that of the world's great wisdom traditions, it is only those that derive from ancient Israel—Judaism, Christianity, and Islam—that make history the context and subject matter of theology. This deep difference between what are called the "Abrahamic" traditions and the others is relevant to the task of discerning what God calls us to do today.

The world's great wisdom traditions arose around two and a half millennia ago. Serious and influential reflection about the difference between custom, on the one side, and truth and rightness on the other, appeared for the first time in various parts of the world. Karl Jaspers taught us to call that period the "axial age." To this day, the ideas and movements generated in that period are the major source of beliefs about the purpose and meaning of life in the civilized world.

It seems that history was internalized into reflection about the meaning of life only in Israel. Obviously, this does not mean that most cultures have had no interest in what happened in the past. In antiquity, and in civilizations everywhere, records are kept about what happens. Stories are told about past events. Further, many stories are explanations of why people act as they do in the present.

Children often come to understand their culture by learning about the first instance of what they now do regularly. The questions may be about why they do or do not eat certain foods; why they prepare them in the way they do; why tasks are divided as they are between the genders; why children are excluded from certain activities. The Jews wanted to know why the seventh day of the week was a day of rest. They told a story of creation in which the Creator rested on the seventh day.

Stories about the past played a large role in creating coherence and loyalty in tribal groups. A Cherokee learned what it meant to be a Cherokee by hearing stories about what Cherokees had done. Which tribes were friends, which, enemies, became clear through stories.

These common elements of ancient tribal life could have developed into historical religions or wisdom traditions. However, in cities that established cultural norms in the past few millennia, this story telling declined in importance. The focus was on accurate description in the present, so as to maintain order over large areas. When profound reflection about the meaning and goal of life arose, it was more often directed to individual spiritual experience. I judge that this is the result of distinctive historical factors, and in this sense all the traditions arising in the axial period are "historical." But history is not built into the beliefs and practices that most traditions adopted.

Consider Buddhism, Jainism, and the great schools of India that together the West called Hinduism. They led the world in the development of spiritual disciplines and of profound reflection on the human spirit and how it is affected by various types of meditation and spiritual practice. They teach how to seek, and often to find, profound inward serenity. The teaching may be that when one rids oneself of all illusions about the world in which one lives, one experiences what is as it is and achieves fulfilment.

Obviously, I am only illustrating an ahistorical spiritual wisdom, but so far as I know, they all focus on what they understand as the unchanging aspects of reality, even if the unchanging aspect they attend to is that everything changes. In China, the Book of Changes analyzes the many types of change that occur. But it is assumed they occur in all times and places. Whereas those of us in the Abrahamic traditions recognize that Moses and Isaiah and Jesus were each speaking to the situation of their time and place, the discoveries of Gautama seem ageless. They do not need to be reformulated just because they were made two and a half millennia ago. The features of human experience with which Gautama dealt are, or at least can be understood to be, unchanged.

In China, Daoism has led to similar results. Also, Buddhism proved very attractive. However, the most characteristic wisdom tradition in China is Confucianism, and, unlike the traditions I have mentioned thus far, it deals with human history. It encourages individuals to find meaning in improving the historical situation. It is thus historical, in a certain sense. It deals with historical structures. Nevertheless, Confucius's intention was to talk about what makes for a good society in all times and places.

It may not be accidental that a Confucian China welcomed the radically historical thinking of Karl Marx. Nevertheless, Confucianism on its own does not go in this direction. Its topic is not radical historical change or how to bring it about. Followers of Marx, like followers of classical American Enlightenment thought, felt it necessary to weaken the Confucian hold on the Chinese mind in order to create the new society they sought.

The Greeks were eminently able to provide information about historical events. They were much better than the Jews in distinguishing what probably happened from the legends about past events that the Jews recorded and read. But their great contribution to human wisdom came in philosophy, understood to include mathematics and science. Here history played no role.

Whereas in India the great thinkers probed the nature of reality for spiritual purposes, in Greece the goal was chiefly secular knowledge. The objects of knowledge were the entities that make up the current world, especially as they are experienced visually. When the entities studied were not the actual objects of sight, they were analogized to them. These entities included the world of invisible forms studied by mathematics as well as the world of physical things. Of course, the human soul came into play, but its role was far less central than in India.

As the term "Indo-European languages" implies, the languages spoken in Europe and in India are similar. Hebrew is not an Indo-European language, and Israel took a quite different direction in the axial period. One difference that strikes the reader is that, whereas the axial thinkers in Europe and India focus much more on seeing, the Hebrews focus more on hearing. They asked, not about God's appearance or about God's visible acts, but about what word one has heard from God. The primary relation of individuals to God is being "called." And even the creation story is about God "speaking" the world into existence.

The focus on hearing encourages the emergence of what Martin Buber taught us to call an "I-thou" world rather than an "I-it" world. In an I-thou world, one does not know in advance just what the "thou" will do. The science and philosophy of the Greeks led to the ability to predict and control. The interpersonal relations of the Hebrews led to constantly changing and developing social events, in short, to history. The greatest achievement of the worldview that developed out of seeing is science, and we know that science attends overwhelmingly to what can be repeated. Historical cultures, however, focus attention on nonrepeatable events.

Even though history is the outcome of numerous, partly independent decisions, generalizations are possible. Also, the way the past is remembered shapes decisions in the present. Distinctive of Israel is that its thought-leaders called it to respond in the present to events that were thought to have taken place some centuries earlier. The most important connection was made between the exodus event and current responsibilities. The Exodus was interpreted as God's gift to an enslaved people. Those people owe their freedom to God, and they therefore owe to God their total loyalty. The recollection of having been slaves in Egypt is the basis for their concern for the poor and oppressed in the present.

The rulers of the Hebrews were, in fact, not all that different from rulers of other people. However, Israel produced a succession of "prophets" who judged the king by standards drawn from history. The king was understood to rule under God, and to be judged by the God who was known through that history.

Some kings did not agree to this subordination of their authority to God's. Some killed those who spoke against them in God's name. But the prophetic belief that God had acted historically in the past was widely influential in shaping expectation and action.

Understanding of the past grounded not only directions about the present, but also hope that God would act in the future. A God who had redeemed this people from slavery in Egypt could act again. During the days of subjection to Roman rule, this meant God could again free this people. God was understood to act typically in and through the acts of human beings. Hence the expectation that God would act again was also the expectation of a human Messiah.

A central question about Jesus's understanding of his mission is whether he thought his role was to be this expected one. If so, how did he conceive the work of the Messiah? In a society that under-stands itself historically, there are likely to be many versions of the history and competing interpretations of its implications for the future. In the preceding chapter, we saw how the message derived from Jesus was transformed by changing historical circumstances.

Both during his ministry and after his crucifixion, Jews debated whether Jesus had been the Messiah. Most thought not, but enough thought he was the Messiah to generate an extraordinarily successful missionary movement. Many of its early converts were Gentiles who participated in Jewish synagogues but could not be fully accepted by the Jews because the males were not circumcised.

Here, again, the issue was history. The story of Abraham explained that his progeny would be distinguished by circumcision. Paul, as a Jew, lived out of this story. He could not dismiss the importance of circumcision from a purely rational or spiritual position. He did so through claims about history.

Paul believed that the Messiah brought in a new historical epoch in which physical circumcision was replaced with spiritual circumcision. What is really required is "faith" or "faithfulness," rather than obedience to rules, even the defining rule of circumcision. Those who followed Paul, or who came independently to similar conclusions about the new covenant or testament inaugurated by the Messiah, opened the door of the new branch of Judaism to uncircumcised Gentiles. To be part of this new movement was to appropriate the history of Israel in a particular way, based on the affirmation that the Messiah had come

The Christian canon is organized in a way that reflects the universalization of this history. It begins with creation and ends with the End. We Christians locate ourselves in the period in which the Jewish community was opened to Gentiles, that is, to all, and before the hoped-for fulfilment. The history, formerly claimed only by one people, is now broadened to express God's dealing with all humanity. Understanding ourselves in terms of where we stand in this history has been characteristic of Christians from then until now.

I hope that the radical difference of the Hebrew prophets, and those who are informed by them, from the other wisdom traditions is clear. I hope also that "difference" can be recognized without privileging one approach over others. A historical change, very important to participants in historical traditions, is the recognition of the diverse forms of wisdom embodied in the axial traditions.

From the beginning, followers of Jesus recognized the wisdom of the Greeks. Indeed, many of those who became participants in Paul's communities brought an appreciation of Greek wisdom with them. The intellectual life of the early church dealt extensively with the relationship of Greek wisdom to Hebrew scriptures. Although a few Christians, such as Tertullian, pictured them as rivals, most made extensive use of Greek thought in the development of Christian teaching. Augustine provided the greatest synthesis.

The heirs of the Augustinian synthesis for many centuries viewed this catholic Christianity as unique. When serious contacts were made with China, the proposal of recognizing the positive elements in Confucian thought were opposed. In Japan, also, the efforts of some Christians to appreciate Buddhism aroused resistance among other Christians. The dominant forms of Western Christianity remained largely condescending to Chinese and Indian wisdom traditions until the twentieth century. The now widespread recognition that they have much to contribute has required deep theological changes. Finally, the ecological crisis has opened Christian eyes to the indigenous wisdom that had almost universally been dismissed as "primitive."

These recent historical changes make clear that defining Christian theology as the beliefs codified in any past period is to misunderstand Christian theology as ahistorical. Of course, many Christians have done so. But these efforts have gone against the grain. The heirs of the prophets, including Jesus, constitute a historical community always in transition. Identifying Christian doctrines is never a simple matter.

The reader may be puzzled by the absence of the word "religion" from this chapter. Discussions of the relation of Christianity and Buddhism are often cast in terms of two religions. I want systematically to avoid that. Such an approach assumes there is a category, "religion," on whose meaning we can agree. When we then approach Buddhism as an example of "religion," we already know basically what we are dealing with. At one time, the word "religion," as used in the West, was so closely tied to theism that scholars had to find something in Buddhism that played an analogous role. This can only distort matters. Further, "religion" was so bound up with beliefs in the Western mind that scholars had to articulate Buddhist doctrines. Again, distortion.

This does not mean that nothing in Buddhism bears any resemblance to the Christian God or Christian doctrine. It means only that bringing Western categories derived from the Abrahamic traditions to the study of Buddhism misleads. This does not exclude the finding of analogies. There are resemblances between the role of Buddhism in Buddhist cultures and the role of Christianity in Europe. Both propose that they are offering a normative way of life and understanding. I have on occasion proposed that we consider the "great Ways" as a rubric. Here, I have talked about "wisdom traditions" as a fairly neutral and nondistorting category. This also has the advantage of clearly including Confucianism and Greek axial thinking.

Another reason for setting aside "religion" in reflecting about the most fundamental characteristics of our history is the fact that while the connotations of "religion" have been largely derived from the Christian form, these connotations do not apply to the founders from whom the church draws its normative models. The prophets were very critical of the religion of their day, which consisted of ceremonies, sacrifices, and feasts. They did not intend to replace it with another set of ceremonies, sacrifices, and feasts. They urged instead that justice be done, and God's will be fulfilled. Jesus clearly fits this prophetic model. When Christianity is considered chiefly under the rubric of religion, its internal norms and goals disappear.

The most important theologian of the twentieth century was Karl Barth. He denied that Christianity was a religion. Many people are doubtful that Confucianism is a "religion." Most exclude Greek philosophy from the category of religion. Few representatives of Indian spiritual religions like having this category imposed on them. It is time to set it aside, except when we are focusing on cultic activity such as feasts and festivals, ceremonial events, and personal prayer practices. These are important in many individuals and societies, but in this book, they are not in focus.

☀ 4 ☀

THE FADING OF HISTORICAL
CONSCIOUSNESS

CHAPTER THREE makes the case that the Abrahamic traditions are radically historical in character. That is, history is built into basic teachings and attitudes, and norms are derived from what has happened in the past and from what past events lead people to expect in the future. New historical events and circumstances call for new developments in these traditions. They are unique in this regard. They express and encourage historical consciousness, that is, understanding every human event as occurring under particular historical circumstances and being largely determined by them. However, for historical consciousness, it is very important that "largely determined" never entails "wholly determined." God is emphatically not in control, even if God plays an important role. History is not the inevitable unfolding of what has happened. It is full of novelty, but the novelty that occurs is the novelty that is possible given the specific personal, natural, and historical context.

This way of understanding ourselves and our world came into being historically through Israel. Sadly, there is no assurance that even the thinking produced in this historical tradition will itself embody historical consciousness. Many Christians try to find an ahistorical essence in Christianity or a set of ahistorical doctrines that express what all Christians should believe at all times and places.

Historical thinking works against fixed dogma and any sense of finality. Conservatives, almost by definition, want settled certainties. The ideas of inerrancy of scripture or of certain papal teachings are an effort to prevent, or at least to limit, historical thinking. Fortunately, this effort has never been truly successful. Even the most conservative Christians have recognized a succession of covenants and have anticipated a future different from the present.

Thinking of theology in this way and seeking to discern the implications of historical events anew in each period requires "historical consciousness." For Christians, the historical coming of Jesus has been the focus of attention during much of Western history. Historical methods of research were honed in the nineteenth and twentieth centuries around this topic. The Bible expresses and encourages this kind of historical consciousness. When it is read with that consciousness, it can be a rich source of wisdom and guidance. When it is read without such consciousness, the result is dogmatism, triviality, confusion, or worse.

A person who is not shaped by historical consciousness, if asked what discipleship should be, is likely to answer that it is believing what the master taught and obeying his commands or conforming to church teaching. If some of the beliefs and actions thereby required seem impossible or irrelevant today, the answer might develop a minimal list of beliefs and actions required at all times and places. Without historical consciousness, that is the natural way to view discipleship. These days, the extreme demands of the Sermon on the Mount are typically explained in ways that make them fit fairly easily into a comfortable middle-class life. This simplification may be almost necessary in order to maintain middle-class churches, but few people with historical consciousness would think that it expresses the full meaning of Jesus's own call for disciples.

Those who lack historical consciousness are likely to miss the historical character of Jesus's teaching. For example, I spent some time talking about what I judge to have been Jesus's expectation of the effects of going a second mile with the soldiers who were authorized by Rome to demand one mile of service from any Jew. Against Jesus's teaching it is pointed out that relating in such a way to Nazi guards would not have worked. But Jesus was not trying to teach a set of practices for all people in all times and places. Love of enemy will find very diverse expressions according to who the enemy is and the contextual circumstances. Jesus was addressing a specific historical situation and proposing a practice that might have worked then and there between oppressed Jews and oppressed Roman soldiers. That there are times and places where "going the second mile" would not work is not relevant to Jesus's historical judgment.

Another possibility for those who lack historical consciousness is similarly to begin with the notion of exact obedience to every moral teaching of Jesus, but then move in a quite different direction. Some Christians have decided that when we try to obey Jesus, wholly and literally, even in imagination, we recognize our inability and thus the depth of the control of our lives by sin. We are then prepared to confess our radical sinfulness and to place ourselves in faith in the merciful hands of God. In a sense, we abandon the effort to be disciples of Jesus and, instead, supposedly in the writings of Paul, find the good news that Jesus's death atones for our sins. Believing this replaces discipleship.

Paul would be distressed by this interpretation of his message. If we read Paul with historical consciousness we understand that he was a faithful Jew who understood that, in Jesus, the messianic expectations were transformed and fulfilled. The law was no longer applicable. Love replaced law as believers participated in the life, death, and resurrection of Jesus. But historical consciousness also enables us to see that the meaning of Paul's teaching *for us* is not identical with its meaning for Gentiles and Jews in his day.

My point in all this is to accent the crucial importance of historical consciousness for Christians today. Without it, my quest to understand what it means today to be a disciple of Jesus could have no valuable outcome. This consciousness was central to the Hebrew prophets, to the Jews of Jesus's day, to Jesus, to Paul, and even to the Gentile converts. But it may be even more important for us today. Without it, Christian "faith" makes no sense and may even work against real discipleship.

Many thoughtful observers find contemporary Christianity irrelevant to the real needs of our culture. My judgment is that they are mistaken, that progressive Protestantism, for example, does have relevance. But usually, when progressive Protestants claim relevance, this is little more than the claim that they join with other progressives in working for worthy causes. Unless we can show that we have a unique contribution to make, we will rightly continue to be ignored or marginalized.

I am proposing that our historical consciousness is a truly important contribution, but few progressive Protestants are even aware of this gift of our past. Many are turning to the ahistorical spirituality of the East in quest of something more practical and relevant to their personal needs. Historical consciousness used to be shared by the educated secular public. Now that it is fading in the secular world, it tends to fade also among liberal Christians who have largely lost the understanding of the unique importance of the Bible. At just the time when historical consciousness is most needed for the salvation of the world, liberal Protestants are ceasing to share it.

Those who have erased this mode of consciousness do not know what they have done. They cannot understand the deep historical change they have caused. With the erasure of historical consciousness has come a great reduction in the study of history. Of course, history is still taught, but, as with other fields, what is sought in the study of history is not guidance for life and understanding of ourselves, but increased factual information about past occurrences. Viewed in this way, Hebrew history has no more importance than that of any other people, and the story of Jesus is of no more interest than thousands of other stories. Theology has no purchase. And no truly helpful alternative is offered.

However, we still have a chance of making our distinctive contribution. Some moderns are recovering awareness of the need for stories. This opens the door to telling credible Christian stories about world history. They might replace the incredible ones with which Christians have too often contented themselves. We can, like the Bible, expand history to include the cosmic story. It can include God's role and the hope that it offers for the present and future, informed both by how Christians have experienced God and by what science has recently learned about the finetuning of the universe. The story can display the centrality of Jesus. And it can include the history of the church in its real importance, both in its terrible distortions and in its quite remarkable achievements.

We Christians can gain understanding from the truthful and comprehensive story about who we are, our faults and limits, but also about our unique opportunities to contribute to the salvation of the biosphere. Part of that contribution will be the story itself and the historical consciousness it expresses and encourages. We will no longer allow the dominant secular mind to inhibit us from offering our self-critical claim to have important contributions to offer. We will be able to call convincingly for a return to historical consciousness.

I am arguing that the world needs a credible, true, and meaning-giving story. The Abrahamic traditions offer examples of such stories told in remote times. I believe that, in the task of re-telling the story in this postmodern period, Christianity offers the best resources. Judaism has not freed itself sufficiently from connection with the story of a single ethnic group. Islam sacralizes the Quran in a way that limits the telling of the quite different story that is now needed. Of course, many Christians have similar limitations. But we have examples of broadening and extending the story. Augustine's *City of God* is a widely accepted and respected example. In the modern world the relevance of other traditions has increasingly been recognized and has affected the way the story is being told. We have been so thoroughly buffeted by the modern world that we will be less tempted to repeat what worked in the past.

When a post-Christian secularity became dominant in the West, historical consciousness did not diminish. Both Christian and secular scholars worked hard to distinguish history from the legends that have played so large a role in Christianity. New secular stories were told about a history of which earlier Christians had been ignorant. Typically, moderns divided history into periods, such as: primitive, civilized, classical, medieval, and modern. The idea of a comprehensive overarching history gave birth to Hegel and to Marx. Toynbee may be the last major writer to have offered an influential overview. Bryan Swimme, Thomas Berry, and Mary Evelyn Tucker have extended the story to the cosmos. These moves have been promising. But in the second half of the twentieth century, the full secularization of education and research led to exclusion of this enterprise from our leading educational institutions.

I have explained why I believe that, with the loss of historical consciousness in the secular world, Christians are in the best position to tell the needed story. I also believe that, for good, and also for horrendous evil, Christianity has played the most important role in world history. The only Christians who are in position to write the needed story are those who understand this writing as a part of the task of repentance.

The history we need will be Christian. That is, first, it is historical, and, second, it is about what God does as well as about what creatures do. Third, it gives centrality to the prophetic tradition of Israel culminating in Jesus. But it certainly cannot, must not, minimize or marginalize the other great wisdom traditions. The rise and flourishing of Islam will be an important chapter. The story may well recognize that in many ways Islam was superior to the Christianity of its time. Its scriptures were more coherent and less subject to use in attacking others. What it taught was more credible. Indeed, Islam in general may be superior to Christianity in general. My calling for Christians to take responsibility is not because Christianity is superior, but because Christians have been more thoroughly chastened by the struggle with modernity. More of us are more fully liberated from naïve belief in the inspiration of our scriptures.

The reason that the Abrahamic traditions need to provide the inclusive context is precisely because they are historical. Buddhism and the other Indian traditions do not have the resources to locate the contributions of other cultures and movements in a comprehensive way. On the other hand, the story of the world would be incomplete—and seriously distorted—if the historical role of Indian philosophical/spiritual traditions and the wisdom they offer were not given full visibility within it.

The actual history of Christianity includes the wisdom tradition of Greece. That has already been given an honored place in Christian histories. The history we need will rethink the role of the Greeks from the perspective of the total world situation today. It will certainly not minimize their importance. But it will not conceal the ways in which they misled themselves and the ensuing civilization.

China looms ever larger on the world scene; the significance of its traditional wisdom for both past and present grows with it. Daoism is of particular importance today as the one axial tradition that deeply appreciated the wisdom of nature. It may help us also to recover something of the wisdom of indigenous people that has been drastically undervalued in all the other axial traditions.

As Christianity merged in many ways with the Greek traditions, so there have been other important efforts to synthesize, such as the Sikhs and the Bahais. Today our actual history includes two centuries of interaction and mutual enrichment. This is a climactic part of the Christian story.

Equally, and more important than all this, is the inclusion of the economic and political story that is entangled with the wisdom traditions. Particularly urgent for present understanding and action is the story of Christendom's undergirding of Western global imperialism, industrialization, colonization, and economic exploitation. These have led to a vast increase and concentration of human wealth, the globalization of the economy, and its control by private financial concerns. Obviously, today, the economy is important because it is playing the largest role in the pollution of land, water, and air; climate change; the annihilation of species; and the exhaustion of resources.

For people with historical consciousness, that is, for people who understand themselves and their responsibilities in terms of where they stand in the historical process, some overview is essential. The overview requires selection in terms of what is most important and some kind of periodization of history. Of course, any periodization depends on what one judges to be truly important. In the West, at least in the university world, explicit judgments of importance are no longer respected. Hence, fully secular people can no longer write a comprehensive history.

This fading has accompanied the fading of the Bible from real cultural importance. That expresses both the shrinking of the Western church and the decline in real influence of the Bible, even in the church. Since the Bible (with the Bible-influenced Quran) is the only source of historical consciousness, it is not too surprising that its marginalization has undercut historical consciousness. Still, some of us find it surprising that the secular historical consciousness, which emerged from the biblical one and severely criticized it, has not thrived when it has been so far separated from its biblical roots.

These roots were in a culture that thought about the world of hearing more than the world of sight; that is, an I-thou world in which values and facts cannot be separated. The modern university's rejection of values expresses its grounding in the world of sight, which privileges I-it experience and thinking. The loss of historical consciousness, of the world of hearing, and of value-oriented education, go hand in hand.

Although I am emphasizing the seriousness of the loss of historical consciousness, I must also acknowledge that all historically conscious offerings, Christian and secular, are seriously problematic. Many are justifications of the dominance of the powerful, or of particular ethnic or religious groups. Part of the rejection of what we might call "meaningful" history is to put an end to harmful propaganda written in its guise. We Christians, as we undertake to write an overview of history, must recognize and respect the reasons overviews have been rejected. We must be very clear about the perspective we bring and open it to criticism and repeated reformulations. None will be perfect, but hopefully all will be better than the lack of historical meaning that now prevails.

Since I am one for whom historical consciousness appears extremely important, I shall pause here to comment on what I see as a great impoverishment, from which we now suffer, because of its demise. I will do so by way of an example. My choice is from the history of science.

Most current PhDs from modern American universities have very little understanding of what has happened in the past. This may be especially true of PhDs in the natural sciences. They may have studied one bit of history or another and have remarkably accurate information, but they have rarely been encouraged to think just how the events they studied grew out of their context and background and how those events continue to affect what is happening now.

Of course, recent PhDs, like all people, do have some overall

ideas about the past. Among academics, a common pattern is to
view the past in terms of the kinds of information past peoples
have generated and contributed to us. What is most valued in the
universities, and especially by scientists, is science. For many, the
history of science is the history of what really matters. Sadly, however, very few scientists have seriously studied the history of science,
and the history they live and think out of is seriously misleading.
I will comment on an example.

Viewing the past in terms of its anticipation of modern science,
the Greeks are hailed with deserved appreciation and admiration.
They are seen to have founded scientific thinking. But instead of
a sustained development of this, it is supposed, there was a total
loss of scientific thinking when the Roman Empire collapsed. This
was followed by the Dark Ages. The recovery of Greek science in
the Renaissance of classic culture in the fifteenth century paved
the way for modern science, and since then there has been a steady
expansion and advance.

Those who live by the university story I have summarized often
treat the pope's censure of Galileo as a key event. According to
the common account, Christianity disgraced itself and revealed
its enmity toward science when the pope refused to look through
the telescope at the moon, and, instead, punished Galileo for
challenging the Christian doctrines. This incident is taken as
demonstrating that science and religion, at least in its Christian
form, are inherently opposed.

Anyone with historical consciousness would draw very different
lessons from the opposition Galileo faced in the papal court. The
pope had at his court representatives of what was understood to
be the best science of his day—that of Aristotle and his followers.
Aristotle taught that the heavenly bodies were composed of a more
refined matter than earthly bodies.

The pope was visited by a scientist who disagreed with the
orthodox science of his day and wanted the support of the pope

in overthrowing it. The pope did not want to set himself up as judge of a scientific question; so, he called his scientists to deal with the matter. The scientists were told that if only they would look through the telescope they would reject the science in which they had been schooled and the authority of history's greatest thinker. They declined.

One might argue that the pope should have overridden the court scientists and insisted on their agreeing with Galileo, but I doubt that many scientists would like for church authorities to inject themselves into disputes among scientists in this way. If they ever do so, my guess is that scientists would prefer for them to support what is taken as the best science of the day rather than those who call for change. This incident has nothing to do with Christian opposition to science. The idea that the moon is composed of the same kind of matter as the earth is theologically perfectly acceptable.

This was an important historical event. The mainstream scientists delayed acceptance of an empirical, evidence-based call for a change of paradigm. One might learn from this the importance of avoiding too tight a commitment to the reigning paradigm, whatever authorities may be cited in its favor.

This is not the only instance of most scientists clinging to an established theory even at the cost of ignoring evidence. Indeed, this has happened repeatedly. A recent example is the relation of established neo-Darwinists to Lynn Margolis. The neo-Darwinists have been committed to the view that evolutionary developments occurred only by random mutation of genes and natural selection among the resulting phenotypes. Margolis gathered extensive evidence that what may be the single most important step in evolution occurred in another way.

Margolis specialized in studying bacteria. She found that the eukaryotic cell developed by one bacterium swallowing another but not fully digesting it. Indeed, it consists of a symbiosis of bacteria or parts thereof. Her discoveries directly challenged the dominant neo-Darwinian theory and even its underlying worldview. This caused her to be treated badly by fellow evolutionists. Her evidently important research was seriously underfunded. There was a long delay in acceptance of her views despite the strong empirical evidence.

It seems evident that evolutionists, when explaining the role of random gene mutation, should now make it clear that this is not the only way in which important evolutionary developments occur. Sadly, this does not seem to be the case in many instances. Perhaps contemporary epigenetic studies are finally moderating commitment to the neo-Darwinian account. But scientists who tolerate this kind of current resistance to evidence should not tell the story of Galileo with such condescension toward the Aristotelian scientists. I would like to think that serious study of the history of science would moderate this all-too-common self-righteousness on the part of contemporary scientists, and that it would lead them to more openness to change when evidence calls for it. Regrettably, there is very little interest among scientists in the actual history of science. That has been replaced by a very misleading story.

My point is not that scientists are more hesitant to adjust to new evidence than others. Probably their self-description and socialization make them somewhat more open to evidence than most of humanity. I understand that very recently, after decades of rejection by academic psychology, leaders of this discipline have acknowledged that the evidence supports the reality of "psi." This means that parapsychological phenomena can be empirically investigated by scientists. This is cause for celebration. But it also illustrates how great is the resistance to evidence that upsets existing paradigms.

We can all learn from history how resistant people are to giving up ideas and practices to which they are accustomed, and that have worked well. We Christians have much of which to repent. The wisdom traditions have generally encouraged openness to new information, but their adherents are likely to cling to what is familiar. Their failures are widely recognized, and sometimes exaggerated. I have pointed out that even the community which takes most pride in its openness, the scientific one, is composed of human beings who, in fact, act very much like other human beings.

There is another major lesson to be learned from this incident. Modern science did not arise out of the Renaissance. Medieval scientists had been studying Greek science for centuries. Copernicus had operated in the context of Greek science and made major advances in astronomy, but his work did not lead to further advances. The Renaissance did not lead to scientific advance. The breakthrough came because the medieval world had been remarkably fruitful in its technological developments. Galileo's contribution was to use a telescope. After initial opposition, scientists were forced to agree that Copernicus had been right. Major new scientific initiatives emerged. When one understands the importance of technology to modern science, one can no longer dismiss the Middle Ages as "dark."

Modern science depended on medieval technology even more than on Greek speculations. But this was not the only medieval contribution. Serious historical study indicates that the scientific quest for an order underlying a chaotic surface resulted from the medieval belief in a divine creator and lawgiver. Early modern science was a quest for natural laws of whose existence they were assured by Christian theology. The language suggests belief that there is a lawgiver. This medieval Christian belief was shared by almost all the early scientists. A more accurate account of the relation of Christianity and modern science is that late medieval theology, including a Greek-based philosophy, together with late medieval technology, gave birth to early modern science. A revival of Greek philosophical science would not have done so.

The most important reason for hoping that universities, and the scientists who constitute their core, will recover a historical consciousness is that, to this day, modern Western science clings to a seventeenth-century metaphysics long since relativized by philosophers. In dealing with ahistorical scientists, it is very difficult to get attention to this issue. But it leads to trouble in many directions.

The influence of technology on modern science shows up in the language often used in the early days. Scientists thought that everything operated by "clockwork"; so, scientists sought the clockwork that explained the behavior of living things as well as inanimate objects. We call this kind of thinking mechanistic, and Descartes argued that, in fact, living things are complex machines, like the figures that danced around medieval clocks on the hour. The mechanistic worldview became established as the scientific worldview. Despite much evidence that living things are not machines, this metaphysics still dominates science and, after Darwin, has come to dominate the university.

This metaphysics has indeed evoked opposition from the humanistic and Christian communities. It implies that all human beings are zombies, including the scientists. No one really believes that. It has very little support among philosophers. But because of its association with science and the absence of historical thinking, it reigns supreme in our most prestigious institutions. This poses a severe problem for mobilizing people to do radical thinking and radical acting to respond to the radical dangers that humanity faces. We have lost historical consciousness just when we need it most.

☀ 5 ☀

SO, WHAT IS OUR
MISSION NOW?

CHAPTER THREE began by asking the question of the book: What *today* constitutes discipleship to Jesus? I interrupted this apparently straightforward question to devote the rest of that chapter to a discussion of what is meant by historical consciousness and why it is crucial to answering the question. Then I devoted another chapter to noting why we cannot take it for granted today. Now, with all that background, hopefully, we are ready to answer the question.

We are ready to understand that what we are called to do today is not the same as what Jesus called people to do during his ministry. It is not the same as what Paul called people to do in response to the news that the Messiah had come. It is not the same as what people were called to do when the church was the most powerful institution in society. It is not the same as what God called people to do in response to the Industrial Revolution. We are not called to repeat earlier responses. But without understanding to what we are called, and why, we have little guidance in answering the question about us today.

We can learn from the past that the mission of the disciple depends on the situation at the time. When Jesus proclaimed a third way of responding to Roman oppression, there was still a chance of avoiding futile and self-destructive actions on the part of faithful Jews. When Paul testified to the power of the Spirit liberating people from fear and legalism, there was no way that the people who learned about Jesus could directly affect the Roman government. But they could experience the kind of community that gathered around Jesus, and they could be empowered to love one another, and, perhaps, even their enemies.

Today, our situation is more like that of Jesus than that of Paul. This calls for reviewing Christian history afresh. In Chapter Two, we traced the outlines of the major church responses in changing circumstances. These all followed the Pauline side of the choice between Paul and Jesus. But now we need to ask whether there were some, even a small minority, who have understood their calling to be to follow Jesus.

The answer is positive. From time to time some Christians have sought directly to create countercultural communities of resistance. These believers lived by norms quite different from the conventional politics in their time and place. They typically rejected violence against people, hierarchical classes, and unequal wealth. Often those who participated in these efforts were persecuted by the established society and even by the established churches. But some of the Catholic orders also represent this effort to achieve true discipleship, especially in their origins. And some groups who have been persecuted, such as the Amish, have survived. Further, new experiments have been tried in our own time. I would point to Koinonia Farms, a communist, pacifist, interracial community in South Georgia, founded by Southern Baptists, as an example.

I deeply admire both the Amish and Koinonia Farms and the many sects that have struggled for discipleship of this kind. Still, I am proposing something different. I judge that our situation is still closer to that of Jesus. Although the result of his work was to create countercultural communities, his goal was to change the national situation. As we view the threats to continuing civilization on the planet, we may decide that the best response is to create countercultural communities that have a chance to survive. But if there is any chance of changing human behavior in a way that will limit the now inevitable suffering, surely some of us are called to do what we can.

Have there been any instances of attempts to change public thinking and action? Jesus called for such a change in the whole of Israel. Have there been later Christians who have called for changes in the whole of society? The answer is Yes.

My youth and young adulthood were spent in the late days of the Social Gospel movement. Pastors in the northeastern part of the country and in the Midwest were shocked by the suffering of workers and their families in the early days of the Industrial Revolution. They re-read the gospels and were struck by the fact that Jesus's proclamation of the nearness of the divine commonwealth was about the whole society and its structures. They re-read the Hebrew scriptures and saw that the proclamation of the prophets was about justice in human relations. Of course, individuals were called to action by the prophets and by Jesus, but the salvation they were called to work for involved the whole society.

The Social Gospel leaders recognized that Jesus's good news was that such a change was possible. They replaced the gospel of the forgiveness of an individual's sins with the good news that society could be ordered in a way that is far more just. They decided that the good news they were to proclaim was for the whole of society rather than about saving individual souls within or outside the unjust society, or creating countercultural communities for a few devout people.

They certainly called for individual conversion to discipleship, but the mission of disciples was to work for peace and justice in the

world. I derived my understanding of discipleship in this branch
of Protestantism. It generated among the mainstream Protestant
churches an ecumenical movement which, by combining their
voices, made their call for justice more effective. This evolved into
the interfaith movement that is so important today.

Meanwhile, Franklin Roosevelt based much of his New Deal
on the proposals of the Social Gospel; and the readiness of so
many to follow him was due in part to decades of Social Gospel
preaching. Of course, in the middle-class churches, where I heard
this message, it was toned down. There was much more talk than
action. And in the years after World War II, its remnants were
marginalized. Nevertheless, I appreciate its leaders and many of
their followers and largely identify with them.

The Social Gospel focused on class and economic issues and
had a poor record in relation to race, to gender, and to sexual
orientation. It contributed little understanding of the history of
Christian persecution of Jews, although an understanding of the
role of Christianity in paving the way to the Holocaust finally broke
through. The Social Gospel at least prepared Protestants for quite
serious repentance once the reality was understood. It prepared
also for positive responses to other calls for justice and inclusion.

In relation to race, the focus was on the treatment of Blacks
first as slaves, and then through segregation, although most White
Social Gospel advocates counseled patience. Nevertheless, when the
Black community found its voice under the leadership of Martin
Luther King, many White Protestant churches recognized their
failures and gave King needed support. Many of us experienced
the Civil Rights struggle as a new and deeper expression of the
Social Gospel.

After King had succeeded in getting the legislation he sought,
he moved ahead to the fullest expression of the Social Gospel that
has ever played a public role in the United States. He called for
an end to the Vietnam War and of poverty in both the Black and

the White communities. He organized a poor peoples' march on Washington and threatened to camp there until Congress acted. Sadly, his assassination ended this project.

The realization that race is a theological topic of great importance paved the way for other extensions of commitment to justice. The feminist movement has been brilliantly successful in social change. Its effects are intimately personal, but also socially revolutionary. In its turn, it paved the way for the next great liberation, first of gays and lesbians, and then of people with all types of sexual preference. These movements have shown that ordinary Christians are not impotent in relation to the extension of justice. But in the areas of gender and sexuality, the primary leadership did not come from the church. Especially with regard to sexual orientation, to this day the expansion of justice concerns has been thwarted by the legalism that has surrounded human sexuality in most churches.

In these ways the Social Gospel was transformed into liberation theology. Needless to say, much remains to be done in regard to race, gender, and sexual orientation. But even more urgent is work for the poor. Attention to race, gender, and sexual orientation has helped some of the poor, but it has sometimes directed energies away from their needs. As I write, we are witnessing the first serious effort to renew the work to which Martin Luther King dedicated his last years. Surely those who wish to be disciples of Jesus are called to support this new effort at a deeper change in our society.

That I admire the Social Gospel and its climax in King's work and other liberation movements is clear from what I-have said. My efforts to be a disciple give enthusiastic support to all of these. Nevertheless, my analysis of our present situation leads me to define my calling somewhat differently.

The first, and most obvious, limitation of the Social Gospel, even as transformed into liberation theology, is that it remains anthropocentric. I am not interested in retroactively blaming its leaders for this limitation. They were creatures of their time and culture, and ours has been, until very recently, a completely anthropocentric culture. Although the Bible is less anthropocentric than modern Western culture, Christians were no better than others in this respect. But since, in the late sixties, we were awakened to the extremely profound consequences of our anthropocentrism for human beings as well as for other creatures, simply continuing this feature of the Social Gospel cannot be our calling.

I judge that, today, the situation is remarkably analogous to the one Jesus confronted in ways that are relevant to what a disciple may be called to do. In Jesus's day the survival of a Jewish nation, even as a Roman colony, was in jeopardy. The deepest trends that were taking place were leading to national suicide. This led Jesus to very radical proposals of an alternative response for Jews to Roman oppression. Neither his proposals nor those of the Jewish leaders in Jerusalem were followed, and national suicide occurred.

In our day, if one projects the deepest trends that are taking place globally, the prospect is global human suicide. Most of the proposals for avoiding this outcome are obviously inadequate. A disciple of Jesus may envision something much closer to Jesus's proposal. The fact that Jesus failed cautions us that the likelihood of success for us, who seek to be his disciples, may be very small. But there may be no other option that has any chance at all. Perhaps our work, like his, will bring about local communities that are islands of ecological civilization that can survive the storm and begin a process of reconstructing a human world.

This means, in my view, that we need to develop an overview of what kind of global society could avoid the total collapse toward which we seem to be headed. This is very different from listing some beneficial changes that have a good chance of being made, although this is also needed. It is also different from repeating the goals of the Social Gospel and adding concern for the natural environment. Serious reflection about our natural environment requires us to change our thinking radically about human society and about ourselves. This requirement is not so different from true responses on race, gender, and sexual orientation. Our thinking about our world and what it requires demands radical rethinking based on all these changes. We must rethink the whole rather than reduce particular injustices.

Jesus described the divine commonwealth in uncompromising terms because no lesser change would result in Israel's survival. We can learn from Jesus that, instead of a laundry list of solutions to problems, we should develop an integrated and holistic vision of the society we need. We also need a convincing name for the newly envisioned society that alone offers hope for the future. We can then have discussions about more detailed questions and what we must do to achieve this goal.

The most impressive move in this direction thus far is that of Pope Francis in *Laudato Si*. He calls the future world that might make survival possible an "integral ecology." That is a world of interrelated things of which human beings are an integral part. When we understand this, we can develop appropriate agriculture, appropriate economics, appropriate education, appropriate technology, appropriate transportation, and so forth.

The United Nations initiated the use of another name, "ecological civilization," that I personally prefer. The Chinese have taken up this name for their goal. Both terms function globally today much as Jesus's talk of a divine commonwealth functioned for Israel in his day. To simplify, in what follows, I will use the term I prefer. However, I trust it is clear that I am eager to be in alliance with the pope, and with many, many others, who are contributing, in hundreds of different ways, and with very diverse language, to the ecological civilization it is my mission to proclaim.

6

WHAT IS ECOLOGICAL CIVILIZATION?

ALTHOUGH THE TERM "ecological civilization" was used first in United Nations literature about the Earth Charter, it has come into wider discussion in this country from China. It came into prominence there when rapid industrial growth led to terrible smog, and to pollution of soil and water as well. The inhabitants of many cities, including the capital, protested these evils. The Communist Party wanted to assure the citizens that it understood the importance of their concerns. The leaders insisted that they could continue industrialization and overall economic growth in a way that would take environmental concerns seriously. To accent this, they wrote the goal of ecological civilization into the constitution of the party. Recently, it was written into China's national constitution as well.

Ecological civilization unquestionably pointed toward environmental concerns and serious commitment to respond to environmental problems. Whether it meant, or would mean, more than this was not immediately clear. However, the term suggests, if it does not necessarily imply, deeper meanings. Some of these are unfolding. I will unpack these implications from my own point of view. What I say has not been rejected by the Chinese government, and in some cases has influenced policy. But China has not committed itself to all of this, and even though some of these ideas may be viewed favorably, no one would claim that most of them have been extensively implemented.

In my view, the term "ecological civilization" calls for unpacking into ecological agriculture, ecological forestry, ecological fisheries, ecological villages, ecological cities, ecological education, ecological psychology, ecological economics, ecological energy, ecological business, ecological legal system, ecological health care, ecological society, ecological technology, ecological transportation, etc. At least, in China, there is interest in thinking about such matters even if the actual results go only part of the way.

For example, if one calls for an ecological economics, thus far the result has been that provincial governors, who were once evaluated almost exclusively by their success in stimulating economic activity, are now also judged, quite seriously, by the effects of their policies on the health of the environment. I celebrate this change.

However, in evaluating the economic changes, the government continues to use the GDP measure that is favored by global capitalism. It gives positive credit for changes that are in fact negative. If an explosion destroys a block of city buildings, nothing is subtracted. However, the rebuilding adds to the GDP. It may happen that what is rebuilt is inferior to what was destroyed. Even so, the whole process is evaluated as a gain. Another example of its misleading character is that nothing is added to the GDP for a mother's care for her children. On the other hand, if she gets sick and hires someone else to care for them, the GDP goes up, even if the childcare is not as good. Measures have been developed that subtract the losses and consider the sustainability of the economic activity. They are not accepted in the capitalist world, because they might restrict the profits of corporations, but China should not be bound by that consideration.

Ecological health care is an area that is growing all over the world. For decades, during the global modernization period, traditional medicine was rudely ridiculed and excluded. Chemistry was king. Obviously, this modern medicine can be credited with many accomplishments. But today the public is aware that focusing on it to the exclusion of other considerations has had negative side effects as well.

I can testify that there was a period, perhaps reaching a high point in the Fifties, when antibiotics seemed to be the way to cure many ailments and prevent many diseases. Gradually it was realized that the extensive use of this medicine was leading to the evolution of new bacteria that could create increasingly difficult problems. Furthermore, many of the bacteria being destroyed were ones the body needs. Antibiotics have their place, but a more limited one than first thought.

There is now much greater appreciation of traditional herbal medicine, of the relation between physical and psychological health, and of the importance of healthful food and lifestyle. In other words, more than on most topics, a holistic view is taking hold. People understand the connectedness of things as they relate to health. Recognition of what is involved here may lead the way into an ecological civilization.

At the time the Chinese Communist Party adopted the goal of ecological civilization, China planned to modernize agriculture. To "modernize" meant to industrialize. Industrialization of agriculture in the United States has led to the destruction of numerous villages and the disappearance of many towns that once served the rural population. It makes farming increasingly dependent on fossil fuels, insecticides, pesticides, and chemical fertilizers. Once the Chinese government reflected on the implications of the goal of ecological civilization, it saw that industrializing agriculture cut against this goal. The national policy shifted to rural development. There are still many problems, economic, ecological, and social, but

the change of policy is serious. In 2016, for the first time, more
people moved from Chinese cities to rural areas than from rural
areas to cities.

This does not mean that Chinese agriculture is now ecological.
It does mean that the possibility of moving in that direction is
still there. The eco-village movement and the organic agriculture
movement are leading the way. It is at least possible that, in a few
years, one will be able to see the emergence, at least here and there,
of genuinely ecological rural life and agriculture.

Ecological farming can be supported by ecological eating.
There are some programs in China connecting urban customers
to rural producers. Unfortunately, as prosperity spreads, meat
becomes an ever-larger part of the diet. This is bad for health. It
also makes it impossible for the nation to feed itself. Meat production requires much more land per calorie than raising plants.
Since the demand for meat is increasing, the Chinese government
is seeking land abroad on which to produce it. Parts of Africa are
being bought or leased, and it is not hard to predict that Africa will
have increasing difficulty feeding its own people. Land is procured
in the Amazon basin where already the world is losing its most
important lungs. For China to move toward being an ecological
civilization, the primarily plant-based diet of traditional Chinese
cooking will have to be retained or restored. The Chinese will be
healthier, and China can play a more humane role in the world.
But what will happen remains to be seen.

With respect to ecological cities, the situation is like that with
respect to ecological economics. Environmental concerns play a
large role in urban planning and in agriculture. However, changes
in the nature of cities, that is, building ecological cities, has not
happened. My understanding of what that would mean is derived
from Paolo Soleri, who proposed "architectural ecologies," or "arcol-
ogies." He showed that three-dimensional cities could be built in
much smaller spaces. People who lived and worked in these cities

would not need to commute to work, and there would be no place for motor transportation. These cities could be operated entirely by solar energy and could even produce much of their own food.

Soleri showed that we have the technology to construct such cities. They could vary, from cities of a hundred thousand to millions. The minimum is a population that can support the whole range of needs of urban living: health care, education at all levels, varied jobs, recreation, many choices of goods for purchase, with most of them made locally. The point is that every part of the arcology is accessible by foot and reached in a short time. The building will contain elevators and escalators and moving sidewalks. Of course, people can go out of the arcology to obtain what is not available within, but if this is so frequent that one would think of acquiring a car for this external activity, the arcology will not be succeeding.

Thus far, there has been very little progress toward ecological education. To make the educational system ecological would require clear articulation of a new goal of education. Ecological education would, of course, be designed to support the flourishing of ecological civilization and prepare individuals both to flourish in those civilizations and to contribute to them.

One change would be a shift from competition to cooperation. Chinese schools, even more than American ones, socialize students into viewing each other as competitors. Since teaching is mostly preparing students to succeed in standardized tests by doing better than other students, there is no escape from competition. Sadly, doing better than others is largely a matter of memorizing more information. The pressure on students is such that they end up considering learning, which should be a great delight, a heavy burden. An ecological education would generate community among students and let them experience how they can all accomplish more with greater enjoyment when they work together than endlessly compete.

The topics on which they should work together would be ones that they consider important. They may make mistakes, but education for ecological civilization will teach responsibility and encourage experiment and entrepreneurship. Students will be encouraged to develop their own values; their own sense of what is important. They will experience how study can deal with real problems and increase relevant knowledge of how to deal with them.

Ecological civilization will also require changing attitudes to the natural environment, including the animals with which we share it. Nature can be brought into the class environment, and schooling can take place in the great out-of-doors. Caring for animals can be just as educational as dissecting them, and what it teaches may be more important. I frequently assert that the socialist society at which China aims cannot be built on an individualist, capitalist, educational system. We can add, an ecological civilization cannot be built on anthropocentric schooling. Students need to experience themselves as participants in ecological systems.

Of course, an ecological civilization also makes judgments of guilt and innocence and of what to do with the guilty. Society's task should not be to punish but to "correct," that is, to bring the criminal back into the community. Judgments about how to deal with a particular criminal might be made jointly by elected officials directly responsible to the community, and by members of the court. Ideally, incarceration should be physically in the community into which the criminal will return, and the prisoner will be made to feel a part of the community to whatever extent is possible. Connections with other members of the community will be continuous and every effort will be made to make reentry as easy as possible. The prisoner will be given opportunities for schooling and learning a trade.

Of course, experts in psychology will be consulted, and they will be asked to help in the process of healing those who are ill.

However, if it seems that there is no way of restoring the criminal to life in the community, then he or she will be permanently incarcerated, but not in a punitive way. Life will be made as good as is compatible with protecting the community.

I have not discussed the possible need for punishment. Some form of punishment may be beneficial at times. More often, if the criminal is in a position to compensate an injured party in any way, this may be helpful to both, even if it is very costly to the guilty party. But there may be cases, for example, when a man has raped and killed a young girl and shows no remorse, that the girl's family will not be able to accept the lack of punishment over and above incarceration. The community may share the parents' feelings. A healthy community will be sensitive to the needs of all parties. There is danger in allowing popular feeling to determine outcomes, but there is also danger in absolute rules that prevent action that may be needed for the healing of victims or for the community as a whole.

It should be obvious by now that by no means would all of my views be shared by everyone who is concerned, as committedly as I, to develop an ecological civilization. Even discussion among such people is still in its infancy. To make statements about a penal system with as little knowledge or experience as I have had is a very uncertain matter. The fact that some disagree with me on any issue need not mean that their views are less appropriate to define ecological civilization than mine.

However, I hope this would not mean that ecological civilization loses all definiteness and distinctiveness. I will articulate two basic convictions that are essential to anything I would call by this name.

1. *Relationality*. Whereas our society understands things largely in their separateness and individuality, an ecological civilization is based on the view that things are deeply, intrinsically, related. Anything called an ecology has

this character. When we refer to human institutions and relationships, the way I emphasize the kinds of relations that warrant including as "ecological" are indicated by the word "community." That terminology is certainly not required, but attention to relations that are cooperative and mutually supportive is. If there are people who are not part of any community, we do not have an ecological civilization. If there are people for whose fundamental well-being no one takes responsibility, then there are people who are not part of any community. The more fully basic needs, including basic psychological needs, are met for all, the healthier is the ecological civilization.

2. *Integration of human beings into the natural world.* Whereas, to this day, our society's thinking and practice are anthropocentric, an ecological civilization will be one that attends to the whole life system on the planet. Human beings are part of that larger system, and they are not the only part that has intrinsic worth. A position that denies intrinsic value to creatures other than humans is not an *ecological* civilization. On the other hand, the position of some deep ecologists that seems to deny any special status or responsibility to human beings is not an ecological *civilization.* A civilization is a human creation primarily for human beings. The phrase "ecological civilization" is a daring one, some would say, an oxymoron. But we are daring to claim that civilization can be so transformed as to take the natural world with great appreciation and seriousness as intrinsically valuable and can fit itself into the great ecological systems of which it is a part. We are not supposing that there has ever been an ecological civilization. We are claiming that it is possible, and that only this possibility gives real hope for the future. Hence, just as Jesus announced that the divine commonwealth

was at hand and called for profound change of mind, we proclaim that an ecological civilization is at hand and call people to a similar kind of repentance.

I am intentionally describing something utopian. For a vision of society to be utopian is not to be strictly impossible or merely fanciful. But utopian envisioning does not ask what is now doable. It does not claim that the present situation provides opportunities for adopting all its proposals. I am describing a civilization whose global adoption could have prevented the catastrophes that have become inevitable. Even now the adoption of these policies could enable many to survive and rebuild. My strategy is to describe what we need, and only then to discuss whether it is possible to move in that direction. The fact that China has committed itself to this goal means that it is easier to describe steps that really could be taken there. Even though many of them are not likely, I have given some indication of promising developments. Chapter Nine will consider why it may be that now is a time when much could be accomplished even in the West.

7

COMMUNITIES OF
COMMUNITIES

A N ECOLOGICAL CIVILIZATION today must take account of the many catastrophes toward which the world is heading. It can be thought of as the alternative to catastrophe, but, even at best, it is appearing too late to prevent them. Our task may be to consider how to increase the percentage of the global population that survives, and to give guidance to how civilization can be rebuilt in what will be a less hospitable environment.

The feature of an ecological civilization most immediately relevant to these issues is a move to local self-sufficiency. In this respect, rural areas may have a better chance of survival than urban ones. In the case of most cities, it is obvious that the amount of food produced within them falls far short of the needs of their inhabitants. However, cities can work toward food security, and there are rural areas so devoted to monocultures that, despite the ability of the land to feed people, people may starve. Communist Cuba specialized in producing sugar to exchange for Soviet oil on large government farms. When this exchange ended abruptly, the workers did not know how to produce food. Fortunately, there were still family farms that could prevent Cubans from starving. And city people learned how to produce a lot of food themselves.

The Cuban story shows that this is an area in which great improvement is possible. There is danger that a city's need to provide food for its people will not be apparent until disasters that interrupt the flow of food into the city have occurred. It may then be too late. But there are also possibilities for encouraging a great deal more urban farming and home gardening. There are even examples of small-scale home food production that show it can be a major resource.

The problem may be that people respond to current and readily foreseen needs much more than to less certain future disasters. But here we can appeal, as in China, to issues of health. We know that much of the food in our grocery stores includes poisons, and that, in any case, it has less food value and poorer taste than what can be grown organically in home-gardens. The larger the role of local organic food in our diets here and now, the better for our enjoyment and health, and the more future disaster can be mitigated.

Some people can also be motivated by other environmental advantages. The more we know of the history of the food we buy, the more we will understand how much energy, including energy from fossil fuels, has gone into its preservation and transport. When we combine this with the insecticides, herbicides, fertilizers, and fuel for agricultural production, we will see that growing some of our own food is a real contribution, right away, to the future habitability of the planet, including slowing weather change.

Local production of energy will have similar advantages. Many people are already using solar panels to produce energy for their homes. It is also possible for local communities to produce a lot of energy collectively. No form of energy is impervious to disruption, but locally produced energy will greatly ease problems when the grid breaks down. Puerto Rico illustrates the suffering caused by storms destroying the systems of energy distribution, the long delays in repair, and the resultant suffering. We hope that what is now built will provide energy locally.

When the global and national systems of economics break down, local communities can still find ways to create money or substitutions for it. If problems do not force us back on such local facilities, public banking at the municipal and even state level in the United States may survive far better than the complex global web of which Wall Street banks are part. In any case, we will all be better off as we gain more independence from the private banking system—to which even national governments are now subservient.

These comments illustrate a general principle of ecological civilization. It holds that basic decisions should be made at the smallest level capable of doing so and enacting them. This cannot be, of course, an absolute rule. There are times when local decision-making is so bad that higher levels must interfere. For example, basic decisions about raising children should be made by parents. Interference, even by the extended family, should be hesitant and as moderate as possible. But this does not give the parents complete freedom to beat and sexually abuse their children. Alongside decision-making by the most local authorities available, there must be some supervisory capacity to limit the abuse of power by locals. Clearly, no legal system will ever be free of the risk of distortion.

Nevertheless, in general, local communities, city neighborhoods, or rural villages should be encouraged to take as much responsibility for themselves as possible. The amount of responsibility they can take is greater if they are largely self-sufficient economically. If they are not, many decisions need to be at a higher level, sometimes much higher. Hence the preference for local independence in energy, food, money, employment, and housing. Also, whatever goods can be produced at lower levels should be produced there.

The goal at the lowest level is to relate to one another supportively rather than competitively. Mutual responsibility should be maximized, although not at the cost of personal privacy and self-determination. Individuals flourish when they are part of a community or of several communities. Their personhood is enhanced. In an ecological civilization, individuals are viewed as "persons-in-community." In general, an individual's life is improved more as the community becomes healthier, rather than by a rise in the individual's competitive status within the community. Economies should be designed to strengthen communities.

However much we emphasize the importance of local communities, these will always be parts of larger groupings. Just as it is important to have a collaborative spirit among persons in local communities, so it is also important that communities work together for their mutual benefit. We can speak of the next level up as a community-of-communities. In the United States, these might be counties. We would then move to the level of states, which should think of themselves as communities-of-communities-of-communities. The nation would add a level, the Western hemisphere another, and the planetary organization still another.

Obviously, the existing levels of government are not likely to be the best for this "community-of-communities" model. I use what exists to suggest what is possible now. Once the model is understood, experiments about the best size of communities and communities-of-communities, etc. would be desirable. The boundaries should pay much more attention to natural conditions than to those our anthropocentric past made possible.

The intention would be to counter the tendency to centralize power, a tendency that is built into global capitalism. Nevertheless, it is obvious that we will continue to face global problems that require global solutions. Today, especially at the national and global levels, decisions are made chiefly by corporate entities, especially financial ones. The hope is that in the bottom-up system proposed here, the people will have more control over those who are supposed to represent them.

My belief is that this has a better chance if, at all levels, people vote for people they know or, at least, can learn about in face-to-face relations. This has a better chance if members of the higher-level government are selected by people at the immediately lower one. At the lowest level, for example, in a small to medium-size town, all citizens will participate in the election of town officials. These officials will select those who will represent them at the next (county) level. The elected county officials will select the state officials.

No system will eliminate corruption altogether. But the elections envisaged here will be much less expensive and, therefore, much less controlled by wealth. Locally, people will be more likely to trust their personal knowledge of the candidate and be less swayed by advertising whose purchase is expensive. When they vote for those they know personally and whom they have reason to respect, the chances are better of rejecting people who will serve corporate or personal interests instead of the voters. There is a chance for business to function for the community rather than control the community for its benefit. When these locally elected officials select representatives for the next level, these should be people these officials know and trust. One may hope that they would really care about the lower-level community they represent. Their reelection would likely depend on how the leaders of that lower-level community viewed them.

Despite these advantages, there is always the possibility that one company or individual will gain political control of a town or some other level of government. Provisions need to be made to intervene in extreme circumstances, presumably through the courts. And, of course, the courts can also be corrupted. We can only hope that the people will provide the vigilance and courage to preserve governments that serve the people. As mentioned, the legal system would have the task of oversight and intervention when corruption of the democratic process is dramatic.

8

ECOLOGICAL ECONOMICS

A CHRISTIAN COMMITTED to ecological civilization must consider what are the now most powerful forces that resist and oppose it. This could lead to an analysis of the locus of power in today's world—studying American imperialism and its ties to the dominant financial institutions. But that would be another book. We will take time here to ask about competing ideas, and especially those that support the institutions we most oppose. This leads to recognition that the dominant forces shaping world society today are economic, and that economic theory plays a major role in directing and justifying the dominant policies. Current economic theory rejects the two points made at the end of Chapter Six and encourages the concentration of power at the global level. As long as this theory controls education and public policy, real progress toward ecological civilization is not possible. We need an ecological economic theory to replace the now dominant, highly unecological one. This chapter will briefly summarize the history of modern Western economic thought and note the effects of being guided by it. Then it will sketch an alternative economic theory.

The father of modern economic theory is Adam Smith, who

also wrote a book about ethics based on sympathy. Sympathy encourages action for the sake of others, even when this action does not directly benefit the actor. However, Smith was impressed by the fact that, in the marketplace, there was no need for sympathy. Indeed, the market would not work well if it depended on sympathy. When one goes to the store to get meat for dinner, one does not want to have to appeal to the state of mind of the butcher. It is far better that the transaction benefit him. Indeed, the market is a wonderful institution for win/win relationships.

The butcher wants the money more than the meat. You want the meat more than the money. Thus, trade is beneficial to both partners. People will not engage in trade unless they benefit. The more they trade, the more they benefit. Therefore, the increase of market activity is inherently good. The goal of economic theory is to increase this activity and thereby benefit society.

Obviously, there are dangers that the market will not work well. If someone urgently needs a medicine, and there is only one supplier, that supplier can charge an exorbitant price. It is important that there be competition among suppliers. In a healthy market, customers can choose from alternatives according to price and judgments of quality. The competition among sellers is incentive for improving quality and efficiency of production. Monopolies must be avoided. Government action may be needed.

Another distortion can arise if there is deception. Adam Smith was thinking chiefly of a village market. There, he noted that deception would soon be revealed, and the guilty party would lose the confidence of buyers. When the market is large and impersonal, however, there may be a place for government here, too.

Based on these observations, and taking care to prevent the distortions noted, economic theory studies how to increase market activity as rapidly as possible. What it aims to do, it does well. But, notice its lack of attention to the wider range of relationships that are also important.

Economists do recognize that when two parties benefit from trading, there may be effects on other people as well. These may be negative. This may be another place where governmental action is needed. There are many examples. Two corporations may work together to weaken a third. Two individuals may profit from a real estate transaction that reduces property values for others. People expect to be protected by government from transactions that damage them, but current economic theory tends to discourage government intervention. This concern plays a very small role in economic theory and in the policies that economists support.

Although economists emphasize that market transactions are "free," the rich have advantages over the poor. These advantages are cumulative. In every market economy, wealth is concentrated progressively in fewer hands. The concentration of wealth is also the concentration of power, which, in turn, furthers the concentration of wealth. Political efforts to check this growing inequality are generally discouraged in the name of economic theory.

Economists tend to be critical of government ownership, because competition does not work well when government is one of the parties. Currently, in the United States, the national post office, public medical care, public retirement programs, public schools, and public parks, are all under attack on the basis that private ownership is more efficient. Privatizing all these will increase the market's role. Economists trust the growth of the market to make more and better jobs available to the poor. So, they are not much disturbed by the fact that privatization increases the gap in services for rich and for poor. However, the public has reason to be concerned that economic theory supports the attitude expressed in that very influential book, *Atlas Shrugged*.

Now, consider the relationship to the natural world. Standard economic theory views everything other than producers and consumers as resources. Resources have value for the market and therefore for those who trade in the market. But, in themselves, apart from human use, there is no consideration of their interest or well-being. Their value is their price.

In principle, economic theory allows for consideration of long-term profits as well as short-term. But as it plays out in corporate actions, short-term wins. Management is rewarded for the bottom line. That a forest managed and cut on a sustainable basis will improve profits ten or twenty years in the future does not count much in evaluating current decision makers. The reality is that, guided by economic principles, humanity has been exhausting resources at an increasingly rapid rate.

Heightened emphasis on long-term profits would help a little, but probably not much. Perhaps nothing will. But there are millions of people who are beginning to experience the ecosystems of which they are a part as having aesthetic value, cultural value, spiritual value, and value in and for themselves. Turning a forest into a desert may be good for the bottom line of a company, but it is now widely felt as a travesty and even a sacrilege.

Clearly, the economic theory that takes account of these values in nature will be very different from the one we now have. Rather than complicate matters unnecessarily, we can introduce the idea of community. Current economic thinking places no value on human community. It is viewed only as a collection of individuals, and its value is just the addition of the independent values of these individuals. How they relate to one another makes no difference. However, we know that personal happiness or well-being is more affected by the quality of relationships than by the quantity of possessions. Ignoring this has meant that economists have typically favored policies that are destructive of community.

Once we have understood that people are benefited by the improvement of the quality of their communities, we find that, in fact, for many people the natural surroundings of their human community are part of their extended community. Pets are often an important part of the family to which they belong. When a beloved tree is cut down, the human part of the community feels a loss. When the bird population is greatly reduced, the quality of the community declines. When a stream runs dry, what is lost is not only beauty and recreation and fishing, but also a part of the community. An economic system aimed at strengthening this community would work out very differently from one that considers trees and birds and streams only in relation to the quantity of market activity they support.

The difference comes directly to the fore in relation to non-human animals. Most of us recognize that where there are sentient beings, there is value, independent of how we humans value it. The unnecessary suffering of an animal is an evil. We believe that God suffers with it even if we know nothing about it. An ecological economics will have as part of its goal the maintenance of healthy ecologies that support positive experience for all the animals that belong to it. Current theories have led to the manufacture of meat with little consideration of the suffering of the animals raised for food. An ecological economics would not support anything of this sort.

Now let us consider the issue of scale that was the topic of the preceding chapter. Following the guidance of economic theory has an inherent tendency to centralize production and even distribution. Small towns have fewer producers and stores. Most of the stores that remain are franchises of chains rather than locally owned. Population is concentrated in big cities, since that is where the jobs are. The application of standard economic theory to agriculture in the United States has depopulated the countryside.

Let's suppose that, instead of focusing on individuals in isolation from their social connections, we think of their well-being as bound up with the well-being of their communities. Instead of mentioning that third parties may be affected by trade between two people, we ask what policies and what actions by individuals will most strengthen the community.

This would mean that the village or neighborhood took some responsibility for its own development. If it is a genuine community, all will feel concern for all. There will also be concern for the long term. People will want to encourage local entrepreneurs rather than chain stores and restaurants. They will seek to develop their own production facilities. Even if locally produced goods are more expensive or of inferior quality, all will benefit from circulating money locally and employing local people rather than shipping money and jobs to a distant city. The people in the community will work together to encourage greater efficiency and improved quality.

In conclusion, we can see that the methods that lead to the fastest growth also lead to the fastest concentration of wealth and destruction of the environment. Further, as wealth is concentrated, so is power, and that power is used to speed up the concentration. This whole economic theory and the policies it supports should be recognized for what they are, the best means to achieve very particular goals. Attention should then focus on whether those are the goals that are wanted. They are in marked tension with ecological civilization.

If we want to move toward ecological civilization instead of speeding up the concentration of wealth and power, and the destruction of human communities and the natural environment, then we should evaluate "growth" in a very different way. Today, people think that the goal of every country, and of the world as a whole, should be to increase the quantity of market activity. This is measured by the GNP or GDP. A great deal of attention is paid to this statistic.

It would be a mistake to simply give up this measure. It has its value and use. It was originally developed to evaluate the ability of the United States to wage war. It is relevant to that concern, and as long as the United States aims to dominate the planet, those who do not want to be part of its empire will have to prepare for defense.

However, we are discussing our goal. This must include a world that has so organized itself that the dominance of any one country will be excluded, and no country need fear others. This is not pure fantasy. Europe was once the starting point of many wars, some of which became global. Europe so reorganized itself that European countries no longer fear the aggression of their neighbors. When having money for military defense is not important, we can have a world in which what is measured by GNP or GDP is of minor value. People can recognize "growth," as measured in this way, is often accompanied by the decline of the quality of life for most people, and that it is almost always accompanied by a decline of future prospects.

We should not deny that voluntary trade is an important part of a healthy economy. To measure it is worthwhile. But it is equally true that the exhaustion of resources is an economic loss. Currently, there is no subtraction for the destruction of a forest. If there is an extensive fire that destroys much of a city, nothing is subtracted from the current measure. Indeed, the destruction is likely to add to GDP, since the cost of clearing away the mess and rebuilding is all added. Even if the situation remains much worse than before the fire, the GDP will indicate growth. War increases production. The more we bomb, the more bombs we manufacture. This all adds to the GDP. And in the country that we lay waste, nothing is subtracted for the destruction. Surely improvement should be measured rather than the money spent on destruction.

There are many other limitations. If the wife and mother of a family stays home, cares for children, feeds the family, mends the clothes, does the shopping, etc., nothing is added to the GDP for her contribution to the well-being of the family. On the other hand, if she takes a job, hires a housekeeper, buys a second car, takes the family to restaurants, and spends hours commuting, both her wages and the expenditures needed to replace her work at home are added to GDP. We might agree that the well-being of the family may not be much improved, indeed, that it might decline.

Some consideration should surely be given to actual effects on actual people.

It is obvious that the GDP rises equally whether the people all benefit, or the growth is only among billionaires. But to say that a nation in which most people are having a harder time while the very rich are becoming richer is truly improving economically is absurd. Yet that is often the boast today. Surely, in fact, the distribution of funds is as important as the sheer quantity.

Progress toward an ecological civilization requires much more. But, even taking account of absurdities, such as those I have noted, would help. And that would not be difficult. Measures exist that take account of problems of this sort and many others. Even mainstream economists acknowledge that such indices come closer to measuring well-being. But they are not used, and I am not aware of any effort on the part of economists to get them used. We may ask Why? My impression is that the reason for lack of interest in improved measures is that if governments were guided by them, they would adopt policies less favorable to the concentration of wealth and power in a few hands.

9

PROSPECTS FOR
ECOLOGICAL CIVILIZATION
IN THE UNITED STATES

THERE WAS A BRIEF PERIOD in the late 1960s and early 1970s when the United States exercised its global leadership in a way that led toward ecological civilization. Earth Day 1970, climaxed a promising global movement that largely looked to the United States for leadership. Unsustainable features of our national and local practices were identified, and alternatives were given consideration.

In the early 1970s, there was a strong popular movement for restructuring the world so as to make it a sustainable home for human beings. This movement created a climate that caused Congress to pass some excellent legislation. This was signed into law by Richard Nixon. Working for a sustainable society was not viewed as a partisan matter.

The speed with which the sustainability movement grew to political power caught the corporate world by surprise. But by the mid-Seventies it had recognized that the achievements of this movement were not good for corporate profits. The corporate world developed strategies to recover control.

Clearly a direct attack on the goal of sustainability would not be politically wise. The strategy adopted was to fragment the movement. Since the corporations controlled the media, they could change the language without directly supporting unsustainable practices. By the mid-Seventies there was little public discussion of sustainability in general. There were many causes that had been promoted under that heading. Now they were treated in their diversity as competing claims on our time and money. The term "sustainable" was used to describe, not the habitability of the planet, but the kind of economic growth for which the establishment hoped. This corporate strategy succeeded in its effort to renew corporate control. It fragmented what had for a few years been a unified movement with real political power into dozens of causes that could be dismissed as "special interests."

Our presidents could claim to be concerned about the environment and then express that concern in beautifying freeways. They could express concern for the poor and support them by stimulating the economy in ways favorable to corporations. None of the fragmented movements could counter or even expose these hypocrisies. The leadership of the United States globally worked for American hegemony, corporate profits, and increasing the control of most of the world by private banks. Despite some fine rhetoric by Clinton and Obama, the world's movement to biocide accelerated.

The first effective counter-movement gathered around the recognition that, globally, temperatures were rising. The damaging consequences were effectively exposed. Since not every location was in fact warming, leaders wisely changed "global warming," to "climate change." This phenomenon, hardly noticed in the Seventies, had obvious negative effects important to everyone. For many people, it provided a focus around which political action could be generated. Bill McKibben and his organization, 350.org, gave the new movement an attractive and unifying face. Globally, the concern led to the Paris Accords. The United States probably did more to weaken the accord than to encourage the needed action, but at least it took part in the discussion and signed on to the agreement.

Accompanying inaction with fine rhetoric was the rule. The United States prevented serious resistance to policies that were still leading humanity to self-destruction. As I viewed what was happening, I was reminded of the frog that does not resist being boiled to death if the rise in temperature is gradual. Trump ended the hypocrisy as well as the moderation. He turned up the temperature abruptly and shouted from the rooftops what he was doing.

In the United States, where the best that now seems possible is to defend the natural and social worlds from rapid and devastating depravations, describing the urgent need to move in exactly the opposite direction, toward ecological civilization, may be pointless and even seem silly. But my judgment is different. As a people, we realize more vividly than ever before how important are fundamental understandings about the world and about human policies.

One strength of the now dominant forces is that its supporters know just what they want, and they intend to get it. One weakness of the liberal resistance is that, at best, it is mainly just an attempt to save some of what has been achieved in the past. There is little positive vision. The liberal view can correctly point out that what Trump is doing is immensely destructive and dangerous, but its only goal seems to be to get back to the very unsatisfactory position of the past—the gradually boiling quiescent frog. This goal cannot sustain any enthusiasm.

As I write, a particularly clear example of this problem is very much in the news. Trump has pushed forward the enforcement of immigration policies in particularly dramatic and offensive ways. He has accompanied his actions with callous and racist rhetoric. Finally, he has taken thousands of children from their parents. Millions of people are aroused to protest and even to work against the implementation of the policies.

If the goal were to restore the situation under Obama, all these protests and actions might succeed. But the situation under Obama was only marginally less inhumane. Once people are aroused by

Trump to pay attention, that restoration of the earlier situation
may no longer suffice. However, there has thus far been very little
discussion of what policies are wanted.

There is a chance that large numbers of people will begin to ask
why so many people in Central America are leaving their homes,
engaging in a long and difficult trek across Mexico, and beating
on the largely closed doors of the United States. There is a chance
that Americans will notice that it has often been American policies
that have made life desperately difficult for Central Americans in
their home countries. Perhaps many will understand that American
imperialism is responsible for much of the need to migrate here and
elsewhere, and maybe they will demand real change, beginning
with the dethronement of the neoconservatives.

Thus, there is a chance, a slim one, that millions of people
will transform their anger with Trump's cruel acts into support
of a truly alternative vision. Such a vision would have a chance of
attracting positive enthusiasm, even of winning an election. At that
point, we would face the tough political task of enacting changes
that are painful to a significant, and very powerful, segment of
the electorate.

Also at that point, the media that have aroused our feelings
against Trump's policies would oppose any real change. They would
favor the Clinton/Obama style of humane rhetoric accompanied
by imperialist policies. There is a slight chance that those who
seek an ecological civilization would have learned from Trump
the possibility of moving ahead without media support. Much of
what he does in this way is the opposite of what is needed, but he
has also shown that we could deal peacefully with Russia despite
the neocon demand that we treat it as our enemy.

There is another silver-lining. It may be good that we no longer
look to our national government for global, or even national, leadership. We did that under Clinton and Obama. They accomplished
a few good things at the margins, but, basically, they served the

interests of Wall Street rather than the long-term interests of the people. With little protest, the American people have been lulled by skilled rhetoric to accept compromises that continue our country, and much of humanity, on the path to self-destruction. Now there is protest! That is progress.

In this new cultural context, there is far more openness to consider real alternatives alongside the band-aids with which we have contented ourselves in the past. Moving to an ecological civilization is not so quickly dismissed as irrelevant fantasy. Some proposals, such as single-payer health care, despite the opposition of the leaders of both parties, are at last on the table for discussion and voting. That the Democratic leadership is as fully controlled by Wall Street as is the Republican is now made visible for all to see. That, despite the clear indication that the public wants Medicare for all, Congress can barely discuss it, also makes more inescapable the recognition that Congress serves corporations. It may be unlikely, but it is possible that American voters will work together across partisan lines to regain control of our government.

More dramatically, the abandonment of any pretense of the national government to lead has encouraged the acceptance of responsibility at lower levels of government. This, by itself, moves in the direction of my understanding of ecological civilization. But there is more good news. Globally, the mayors of large cities are organizing themselves not only to be a voice, but also to act.

One of the most important obstacles to real progress in the Western world is the power of banks over governments. We all know that the banks have political power, because we know that they have money, and that money plays a leading role in the political world. But the power of banks goes far beyond that. The banks have control of the money supply, and it turns out that this gives them extensive control over the economy. If governments act contrary to their wishes, they can disrupt economic activity drastically. We saw recently how the Greek government, popularly elected to enact policies for the sake of the Greek people, caved in to the banks. China and Russia control their own banks and hence, although far less wealthy, can engage in projects that seem beyond the reach of the United States. The world cannot help but notice that while the United States has not managed to build a track for high speed trains, China has constructed thousands of miles.

The story of how private banks gained control of Western governments is a long and important one that the banks prefer we not know. Perhaps it can be widely disseminated. Unless the governments of the United States and other Western countries take control of their economies from the banks, it is very unlikely that real progress toward an ecological civilization will be possible. in the West. There is hope. As recently as five years ago, one was considered an "extremist" or a "conspiracy theorist" if one brought up this topic. We had been "educated" to know that "politicians" could not be trusted with the power to create money.

The situation has not changed at the national level. Control by the banks through the Federal Reserve is so strong that few congressmen will touch this central issue. Dennis Kucinich tried to get Congress to discuss money-creation by the government, and he was gerrymandered out of his congressional seat by the Democratic Party leadership. Ron Paul tried to have an audit of the Federal Reserve. but even this effort failed. The banks do not want us to know how our nation's finances are managed. Elizabeth Warren is a breath of fresh air, but I am not aware of any current effort to obtain democratic oversight over our financial rulers at the national level, much less to take from them their monopoly of money creation.

Nevertheless, there is some good news. There has been a change at the level of states and cities. Since the Thirties, North Dakota has had a state bank that has helped it to do well financially through thick and thin. For decades, any suggestion that other states might learn from North Dakota's success was taboo. However, due largely to the work of one woman, Ellen Brown, public banking has become a serious possibility in several cities and states, and it is gaining support in the new acceptance of responsibility at state and city levels. Since it is probable that experiments will succeed and ease the problems of the states and cities involved, it is likely that they will be imitated. Public banks at city and state levels may become commonplace.

State banks cannot threaten the unique power of the national banks to create money. But they do make it possible for states to borrow from themselves and pay interest to themselves. This can greatly reduce the cost of public works. Also, a city or state bank is likely to take more interest in local businesses than a national or international one. Since much of past borrowing by cities and states has been from Wall Street, interest payments have syphoned money from the rest of the country to New York. Public banking increases the power of localities over their own affairs and local economic autonomy.

There is a chance that when the advantages of public banking are widely experienced, the American people will demand that the United States treasury take over the role of money creation from the Federal Reserve, which is controlled by private banks. If this happens, and if, in fact, it turns out that the climate of resistance generated by Trump's presidency has played a role, we will owe much to him, whatever his intentions.

I believe that there is a heightened sense of responsibility at the personal level as well. At least, I am sure that Trump's presidency has not ended important individual initiatives. I will describe one such initiative in my hometown of Claremont, California.

Devon Hartman learned that buildings were responsible for more use of fossil fuel than transportation or manufacturing. He knew that homes could be built to have very little need for this. He also knew that most existing homes could be retrofitted so as to reduce this need greatly. The results included more comfortable living and lower utility bills that rather quickly repay the cost of the retrofitting. He organized CHERP to take advantage of this win/win opportunity.

A local inventor developed a solar panel that solved the problem of "hot-spots" inexpensively. He worked with Harvey Mudd College to test and improve his model. That it can make the conversion of sunshine into electric energy substantially less expensive is no longer in doubt.

The standard procedure at this point would be to sell the patents involved to a large company that could manufacture the new solar panels in a centralized location, probably in a country with lower labor costs. The inventor could then retire to a life of luxury. But this inventor wanted to contribute maximally to those who have the greatest need. He joined forces with Devon Hartman.

Devon has long noted that the customers of CHERP are chiefly upper middle class. We all benefit when upper middle-class homes spew less carbon into the air. CHERP has always been a contribution to ecological civilization. However, Devon is far from satisfied. The homes that use the most fossil fuels are the poorly constructed homes of the poor. These are the people who, in the long run, would profit most from retrofitting. Their comfort would be the most improved. But for them, survival from month to month dominates decision-making. They cannot afford to spend money on home-improvement.

Devon saw that if the patents were sold to a commercial manufacturer of solar panels, the cost could be brought down and the move away from fossil fuels accelerated. Some people who have not thought they could afford solar panels would decide they could. But the situation for those who need panels most would not be changed. And the economic effects would further advance the general tendencies of global capitalism. The advantages gained by the purchaser of the patents might put other manufacturers out of business, adding to the concentration of wealth.

Devon and the inventor have come up with a quite different plan. They want the panels manufactured in thousands of localities, strengthening local economies. Both the manufacturing and the installation would provide good jobs for semi-skilled workers. Also, cities would be franchised to manufacture these solar panels only if they agreed to give priority to retrofitting the homes of the poor with almost no charge. This would be costly. However, the additional purchasing power of the poor, whose housing costs are reduced and whose income from good jobs is increased, would compensate the city. The poor, unlike the middle class, spend most of their money locally; so, the economy of the city would flourish.

It goes without saying that this is a radical experiment, and in an overwhelmingly capitalist context, an experiment focused on helping the poor and strengthening local communities, rather than increasing the wealth of the rich, will encounter many obstacles. But I am deeply moved by the commitment, the quality of the planning, and the progress to date. I put it forward enthusiastically as representing the kind of vision and dedication without which humanity's chances are vanishing.

Meanwhile, American control of Europe, the Mideast, and elsewhere has slipped. For decades we have used our power largely to advance the cause of the banking empires and industrial corporations, overriding the needs of people in many countries. Today developing countries increasingly turn to China rather than the West for advice and support for needed projects. That we are no longer the unquestioned leader of much of the world increases the possibility that people in many countries, appalled by the future they face, will choose radical change. As disasters increase and more people feel the existential threat, openness to radical change may increase rapidly. It will then be helpful if there is a considerable consensus about the right changes to make.

The reader may be puzzled about finding a chapter of this kind in a theological book about salvation. It is my hope that those who have read the chapters on historical consciousness will understand. The calling of those who stand in the biblical tradition is radically informed by the situation in which it occurs. It is features of the current situation that have shaped Devon Hartman's calling. I have been providing a picture of essential features of the current situation that shape my sense of calling. It is my hope that this will be helpful to others as well.

❧ 10 ❧

THE DECONSTRUCTION
OF OBSTACLES

WHEN WE TELL PEOPLE about Pope Francis's goal of "integral ecology" or about the Chinese goal of "ecological civilization," many are attracted. They would vote Yes. But when the specific implications become clear, the situation changes. It turns out that people have other assumptions and commitments that drastically limit what they can think and what policies they can support.

In reality, integral ecology and ecological civilization are very radical ideas. That is, they go to the roots of the issues. If the old roots are still there and have not been questioned, the effort to accept the new ideas will not work.

We read in the gospels the story of a rich young ruler. He was an unusually good Jew. He had obeyed all the laws. Still he did not feel whole; something was lacking. He came to ask Jesus what more he needed to do. Jesus must have found him very attractive and promising. His answer was to invite him to join his inner circle, where he would experience the divine commonwealth. But this would require that he divest himself of all his property. As Jesus said elsewhere, one cannot serve both God and money. The rich young ruler wanted to serve God, and he may have realized that Jesus was right, that his attachment to wealth was blocking the wholeness for which he longed. But he had not been prepared to face his attachment to his money. He went away sorrowful.

Attachment to money, now as then, is a major impediment to entering the divine commonwealth. One may be attracted to the idea of working for an ecological civilization and perhaps finding a community that is a foretaste of that civilization, but if one is not free from attachment to wealth, the door remains closed.

Unfortunately, there are many habits of mind that hold sway in our assumptional systems and are part of our deep convictions. One can work on the positive side and only deal with these obstacles as the issues come up. But this often ends in compromise and lukewarmness. It may be better to bring the relevant beliefs to the surface and deal with them in advance. If one's mind is really cleansed of deeply entrenched beliefs that misdirect us, one can allow oneself to hear the assumptions of ecological civilization. They would have a chance to take root. It is worth a try.

The rest of this chapter deals with deep assumptions built into our minds by our Western history. This is followed by a chapter that focuses on beliefs that shape us as Americans. Similar beliefs may shape other modern peoples, but because of American hegemony, we Americans have a special need to examine ourselves.

CHRISTIANISM

The first of the five topics treated in this chapter is Christianism. This differs from the other three quite drastically. This one is inherited from the Medieval period of European history, and it has already been overthrown in the dominant modern public consciousness. But it continues to play a destructive role among Christians. Since this book is written for Christians, I include it and put it first

I trust that it is obvious that I do not see authentic Christianity as "Christianism." This is not a book against Christianity! Some of us seek to serve God and humanity by following Jesus, and we understand that affirmations of Christianity as the only way, or lashing out at its opponents, are seriously distorted expressions of that quest. But Christians have too often absolutized the church or the Bible or what they understand by "God." Christianism is a form of idolatry no better than the many other forms of idolatry that have informed so much of history. Authentic Christian faith frees us from all idolatries. Becoming a disciple of Jesus cannot mean to turn Jesus into an idol.

Sadly, Christianism has been around for a long time. Charlemagne taught his soldiers that they would be rewarded for killing opponents of what he viewed as orthodox Christianity. His reasons for supporting this were political rather than Christian. But the practice gained a position within Christian theology. It fueled Crusades against Muslims and "heretics."

Christianism has been an all too common form of Christianity. We can be grateful that modernity has liberated much of society from it. But it is still a danger in influential circles. It is still an obstacle to be recognized and opposed. We can move toward ecological civilization only if the great moral and spiritual traditions of the world work together. The twentieth century witnessed great progress, but Christianism remains an obstacle not only to the actualization of ecological civilization, but also to an appreciation of Islam as a great potential ally. It prevents a healthy response to Jesus. It works against the needed openness to humble sharing with others in working for today's equivalence to the "divine commonwealth" whose nearness Jesus proclaimed. The other great wisdom traditions have similar dangers and limitations, but Christianism has historically been, and is currently, the greatest obstacle to the realization of the divine commonwealth.

MODERN METAPHYSICS

By "modern metaphysics" I mean the metaphysical tradition that was initiated by René Descartes. It has taken many forms. Most philosophers today repudiate Descartes, yet the influence remains. Textbooks on modern philosophy begin with him, and he set the terms for most of the discussion.

Perhaps the greatest obstacle to deconstructing the distorted metaphysics that still rules the world is that most people, and especially most philosophers and scientists, deny that they have a metaphysics. When one's metaphysics thoroughly shapes the way one perceives the world, it ceases to be consciously chosen. Hence it cannot be discussed. I will try to articulate the unconscious metaphysics that shapes the thinking of most educated modern people, and that is now a major obstacle to progress.

Most modern people suppose that our best source of knowledge of the external world is through sight. "Seeing is believing." Of course, they know that that world is not simply the patches of colors that are seen. Those colors are the colors of something. The "something" is thought of as a substance, something that stands behind or under the colors, that is, what the colors inhere in. This is supposed to be "material" in nature. It is material entities of this kind that science studies.

Thus nature, the world studied by science, is thought of as constituted by matter. Matter cannot be identified visually or by the data of any of the senses. It has no subjective reality. That is, it does not feel or have purposes. It does not exist "for itself." It is not an agent. When it moves, it is because something moves it. Matter cannot change in its nature, but it can and does change in location. The world is composed of matter-in-motion. Nature is like a machine.

Descartes taught that the only exception to this is the human soul. We know ourselves as feeling, purposing, acting beings. He thought the soul is not material at all. This resulted in the acceptance of metaphysical dualism. Matter is metaphysically distinct from, and virtually unrelated to, soul or mind.

Charles Darwin confused moderns profoundly by showing that human beings are part of nature. Since Descartes had taught us to understand nature as matter-in-motion, the implication was that we humans are, in fact, zombies. Many moderns give lip service to this view, but in fact few think of themselves as simply machine-like. Today, many are reverting to the idea that in addition to machinelike nature, including human bodies, there is also something similar to what Descartes called the human soul, "consciousness."

Obviously, modern philosophies are very diverse. A few philosophers have simply denied the existence of matter and held that everything is soul-like, psychic. There are others who say that we should stick to the appearances and not take any position on what is appearing. There are still others who don't want to get into these issues and talk only about language. I cannot survey here the history of modern metaphysical (and anti-metaphysical) thought. I am only trying to identify what became in modern times a kind of "common sense." It affects philosophical discussion among philosophers who reject metaphysics even more than among those who try to deal with it. Our culture remains profoundly Cartesian, despite lip service to Darwin.

This Cartesian dualism leaves open the question of where the line should be drawn. Even those who may verbally limit mind or consciousness to humans are likely to feel that their pet dog is not adequately understood as matter in motion. It seems to have feelings and purposes. Descartes's serious insistence that the dog has no feelings has never become part of modern common sense, but his teaching has, nevertheless, given license to vivisection of animals and to the industrialization of meat production. Modern Cartesian common sense has always been seriously confused.

The problem is not only confusion. It is also that this modern common sense justifies much that is unjustifiable and gives poor guidance in relation to much else. Instead of illustrating this now, I will take up some of the problems in subsequent sections.

Constructive postmodernism calls for the rejection of both pure matter and pure mind. It rejects the mechanistic model and calls for an organic one. Whitehead described his thought as a philosophy of organism. We should note that Whitehead sometimes describes his view as organic mechanism, since in fact a great deal of the behavior of organisms is describable in mechanistic terms. His choice of organism as the deeper reality does not require us to give up the enormous advances science has made using the mechanical model.

Persuading people, including scientists, that they should shift from mechanistic to organic metaphysics opens the door for significant change. It is a first step to intellectual support of an ecological civilization. But by itself it does not effect these changes. This requires detailed reworking of the superstructure in which the Cartesian metaphysical common sense has been expressed.

MODERN SCIENCE

"Modern science" is the science that followed the guidance of Descartes. In the science of the high and late Middle Ages, the most influential shaper of worldview had been Aristotle. He taught that, to understand something, we should pursue four questions: first, what is it made of; second, what is its form, that is, what are its characteristics; third, what made it come into being; and fourth, to what end did it come into being? These are called the four explanations or causes: material, formal, efficient, and final. Scientists have always been interested in the first three causes, but under the influence of Aristotle, in the late Middle Ages, they tended to focus on the final cause. For example, in their study of the human body they wanted to understand the role or function of the liver, the kidneys, the heart, and so forth.

Descartes was convinced that this function was only superficially explanatory. The scientific question was not whether the heart pumped blood and how this made possible the life of the body, but how it did so. That is the question about the efficient cause. What made the heart pump? Descartes insisted that nothing is explained by the final cause. Purposes play no role in nature. Descriptively, we may of course note that the circulatory system could not function without the pumping of the blood, but the task of science is not this description but an explanation of what makes the heart pump.

To ensure that we do not attribute purposes to the heart, Descartes insisted that it functions like a machine. The most impressive medieval machines were clocks; so, scientists sought the "the clockwork" that explained the behavior of things. We do not suppose that clocks have any experience or subjectivity; certainly, they have no feelings or purposes. They are matter in motion, and the task of science is to explain what makes the motions occur as they do.

Modern science was, and is, brilliantly successful. Again and again, it has predicted what had not been thought to be explicable apart from the introduction of natural or divine purposes. It was recognized that modern scientific knowledge had a definitiveness that had been lacking before. Its success was so amazing that moderns have put this science on a pedestal.

Of course, there was always more to study, but the assumption took hold that, in time, science could explain everything. When Darwin showed that we are part of nature, it seemed that the human soul or consciousness could also be explained in terms of efficient causes, that is, mechanistically.

This meant, in fact, there *is* nothing but matter in motion. Ethics, values, morality, purposes, feelings, etc., etc. are fluff. They can be explained along with everything else as science advances.

And science does advance. With its advance comes a vast improvement in technology and thereby in the control of nature. Modernity
is thus a vast gain over what came before. That there has been
progress can no longer be questioned. This has become the modern
assumption.

Now, however, some of us understand real "progress" not
simply as increasing information, prediction, and control, but as
improving the lot and security of the human species. At this point,
the modern understanding of modern science becomes a major
obstacle to progress. The occasional recognition of this fact leads
to asking whether the Cartesian view of nature as purely material,
which bears some responsibility for our endangerment, is, in fact,
needed by science, or even compatible with scientific findings. It
seems not to work well, not only in explaining conscious experience, but also in explaining the nature and behavior of the quanta
of which supposed "matter" is composed.

Interestingly, it turns out that "matter" does not appear in the
actual writings of science. The closest equivalent is "mass." But not
all the entities studied by science have mass. Few deny the existence
of light, but light has no mass. Apparently, if mass is what we
mean by matter, then matter is only one part of the natural world
studied by physics.

Physics offers us a better candidate for universality. It is "energy."
Now, for the most part, "mass" and "energy" are convertible into
each other. But we noted that light has no mass, and yet it has
energy. Clearly the entire physical world consists of units of energy.
One might think that this makes little metaphysical difference, but
in fact the concept of "energy" is very different from the concept of
"matter." Energy cannot be pushed and pulled in the way we think
of matter as being moved. Energy suggests agency, whereas matter
requires some external act in order to change location or speed.

Furthermore, it is not so difficult to think of human conscious
experience as also embodying energy. Just as evolution should

lead us to suppose, the line between human experience and other parts of nature is no longer so sharp. We noted that materialist views of nature lead to either a dualism of matter and consciousness, or a monism of matter or mind, in which no one can really believe. Accordingly, science itself supports the abandonment of the Cartesian view of nature.

Today's science is showing us more and more about nature that does not fit with materialism. Information has become a central concept. Animals, and even plants, seem to behave intelligently and purposefully. Unicellular organisms respond to human emotions. Rejecting materialism and adopting organic models opens the door to including in science much that has been rejected on *a priori* grounds rather than because of evidence.

Indeed, our more openminded study of what we used to call primitive people now reveals that on many counts they were wiser than we. In the West, we slaughtered many women who practiced ancient medicine that involves psychological as well as physical elements. In fact, they were better healers than the modern doctors of their day, who were more "scientific." We now routinely use placebos to give some recognition to the role of subjective feelings that modernity still excludes from having efficient causality. We find that "primitive" people can learn the location of animals, for example, by methods that are not recognized as possible by the modern worldview.

I am saying little that most readers will find improbable. But the dominance of modern thought in our culture keeps all of this at the fringes. The truth is that indigenous communities have beliefs and practices that are superior to ours in terms of developing a sustainable society. At the fringes, a few people are telling us this. But the dominance of modern thought blocks any significant cultural assimilation.

We are taught that our knowledge and understanding are far superior to that of indigenous people. The truth is that we do know a great many facts about the universe that they did not know. We can develop many machines they did not have. We can reshape nature in ways they could not. But an equal truth is that they understood how to live in a sustainable relation to nature. They understood that human beings are part of a community of subjects rather than simply a collection of objects, so that our relations to others, both human and nonhuman, are subject to subject.

Have we progressed? Yes, in some respects. Have we regressed? Yes, in some respects. But to accept the latter view, that ancients had some knowledge we have distorted or lost, is to reject modernity. Such rejection is urgent.

Perhaps even more urgent is the rejection of the late modern belittling of all questions about better and worse. This is the result of materialism, that is, of the absorption of human experience fully into Cartesian "nature." That absorption arose only after Darwin, and even then, it was strongly resisted.

The most important response was that of Immanuel Kant, who offered a new way of understanding dualism: theoretical and practical reason. To simplify, this meant an affirmation of both facts and values, with these investigated in entirely separate contexts. But by the middle of the twentieth century, modernists judged that facts alone are important, that the facts gained by theoretical reason could explain the judgments belonging to practical reason and show that they had played no causal role. They taught that what has no causal role has no importance. Science is the arbiter of facts; so, science alone is truly worthy of respect.

Hence, the modern world in which we live teaches that it does not matter what people believe about the world and their role in it, that human commitment and dedication make no difference. But the same world has no hope of survival unless people are willing to sacrifice some of their priorities for the sake of more important ones. The unwillingness of modern people to even discuss such questions, and their continuing effort to "solve" problems by the activities that cause them, suggests to me that the modernity dominated by modern science may be the most insane culture that has ever existed. The metaphysical assumptions with which science has allied itself are a major obstacle to building an ecological civilization.

MODERN NATIONALISM AND RACISM

We all take a special interest in those others who accept us as part of their group. For hundreds of thousands of years our ancestors lived in tribes, and the members of those tribes identified themselves primarily in that way. Some other tribes were viewed as friendly, but others were threats. These relations could change over time, but one's fundamental identity and loyalty did not.

With the rise of civilization, citizenship in cities took over as the primary identity and loyalty of many. There was often a close connection between ancestral tribal identity and citizenship in a city. Within a city there might be many people who were not citizens. Slavery was common, and usually slaves were from other cities or from tribes that had not settled in cities.

Some cities conquered others and established empires. However, most of the citizens in the conquered cities still identified themselves primarily by their cities, not in terms of the empire. On the other hand, Roman emperors worked hard to evoke loyalty to the empire and to themselves as representing the empire. When confronting threats from outside the empire, many citizens of cities other than Rome did identify themselves with the empire and its culture against barbarians. Most free people in the empire gave allegiance to Rome and its emperor without abandoning identification with the local city.

Earlier in the book, I called attention to the unique role of the Jews. Other ethnic groups revolted against imperial rule, sometimes successfully. Empires crumbled. But the strength and stability of

the Roman Empire was such that most people finally accepted
it. For religious reasons, the Jews did not. They introduced into
Western history the tension between political and religious beliefs
and institutions.

Obviously, during the heyday of the Roman Empire, their
revolts had no chance of success. However, as the Christian sect
of Jews spread and became increasingly independent of its parent,
people of many ethnicities refused final allegiance to any political
authority. Persecution did not weaken this movement, and when
the Roman Empire crumbled, the Christian church turned out to
be the only sustainable institution.

Now, for the first time, an institution not based on ethnicity
or military conquest gained primary power. At the same time, this
institution did not want to assume all the functions of political
governments. It authorized secular rulers to assume political
leadership. Tribalism, nationalism, and imperialism were replaced
to some extent by Christianism. From that time on, the relation
of "religion" and "politics," or church and state, has been a major
issue in Western society.

Of course, power attracts many people, regardless of whether
it is political or religious. Although the rhetoric of the church
never claimed supreme loyalty for its ruler, practically speaking,
the church could be as intolerant of dissent and disloyalty as the
preceding empire. Its wealth also attracted many. So, viewed from
the perspective of original Christian teaching, many leaders of the
church were corrupted by their enjoyment of wealth and earthly
power. There were many protests, and eventually the protest of
Luther gained powerful support from political leaders. The Western
church split.

The habit of understanding oneself religiously remained
prominent; so now many understood themselves to be Catholic
or Protestant. But the political rulers had played a large role
in determining whether the church in a given area would be

Catholic or Protestant. After decades of fighting between Catholic and Protestant princes, they made peace with the decision that political rulers would decide the form of Christianity that would be practiced in their domains. Secular government became dominant. Modern nationalism was born.

Clearly, this move toward regional self-determination was caused by the Reformation. Protestantism supported it in another way. A strong Protestant principle was that all Christians should be able to read the Bible for themselves. However, this could not happen as long as it depended on learning a foreign language, namely, Latin. Few outside the priesthood could read it. Luther undertook to translate the Bible into German. Since the spoken language differed widely from place to place, he had to decide which form of German he would use. Because reading the Bible in German became extremely important, it created a homogeneous language that could unite people who had before spoken many diverse dialects. It also excluded others whose Germanic languages were too different for Luther's translation to be acceptable, such as the Dutch, the Danes, and other Scandinavians. They needed their own translations.

In this way, national feeling was greatly strengthened. If one read Luther's Bible, one was a German. More and more European writings were in the vernacular, so that boundaries were established among readers. Linguistic boundaries tended to become national boundaries. National feeling became much stronger than when all European literature was in Latin. Modern nationalism was intensified.

This modern nationalism meant not only separating Germans from people who spoke other languages, but also a drive toward uniting the German people in one country. By the eighteenth century, nationalism had fully triumphed. One was no longer primarily a Christian or a Catholic or a Protestant; one was German, or French, or Spanish, or Italian. Wars were fought between nations

over issues of perceived national well-being. Control of distant
regions in Africa and Asia was clearly for building national empires,
and rhetoric about religion played only a secondary, and often
supporting, role.

Nationalism tended to strengthen German concern for other
Germans. Of course, there was hierarchy and exploitation within
the Germanic world. But there was little thought of some Germans
enslaving others. There was also some respect for other Europeans.
So, when Europeans set out to exploit the resources of the planet
and colonize much of it, they did not bring with them the slave
labor that would make that exploitation possible. In order to justify
annihilating or enslaving the people inhabiting other parts of
the world, nationalism had to be accompanied by racism. The
inhabitants of Africa, South America, and North America did
not belong to the same race as Europeans. Indeed, they could be
regarded as not fully human, as being human was understood in
Europe. Accordingly, the rights pertaining to European individuals
did not protect them.

Of course, something like racism was already built into
tribalism. Difference in appearance was not irrelevant. However,
in neither the Roman Empire nor Christian Europe did racism
play a prominent role. Modern Western civilization has been the
most racist the world has seen.

On the one hand, nationalism can help to overcome divisions
based on religion and race. Concern for all those who are part of one's
nation can thus be a positive move toward ecological civilization.
However, the same feelings that draw people together in nations
tend to sharpen boundaries over against others. Other nations
are commonly viewed as rivals, and rivalry can easily turn into
enmity. Despite its potential contributions to accepting differences
within the nation, nationalism is often closely involved with
racism. Nationalism is a major obstacle to building an ecological
civilization. Racism is another, perhaps even more vicious.

ECONOMISM

European nationalism led to two world wars in the twentieth century. So, in its European homeland, the dominance of modern nationalism was brought to an end by the formation of the European Economic Community. It is hard to imagine conflicts between France and Germany plunging the world into war a third time.

What caused the European nations to seek a closer unity may have been primarily the desire to avoid further wars. But it is interesting that they stated their unity in economic terms—the European Economic Community. The clearest expression of their unity was a common currency. Giving up control over its own money was the greatest sacrifice of sovereignty on the part of participating nations. We saw the consequences recently when the political party committed to the will of the Greek people was forced to yield to the European banks. The now dominant shared view and practice can be called "economism." Whereas the threat to peace of Western nationalism is diminished, the threat of economism continues to grow.

Of course, the pursuit of individual wealth has played a large role in all societies, at least since the invention of money. But when Jesus said one could not serve both God and wealth, this was not spoken against "economism" as a comprehensive system. That did not yet exist. During the period of Christianism there was much criticism of the clerical leadership, supposedly committed to poverty, for its luxurious lifestyle. On the other hand, during the modern period not only individuals, but also nations, have been avowedly devoted to the pursuit of wealth. This is a step toward "economism," especially because it increased the power of banks in relation to nations. But in its origins, economic theory was justified on the basis of its promotion of national wealth. Nationalism gave way to economism only when national sovereignty was subordinated to the interests of the economic system. I have noted that this occurred, and was publicly announced, in the formation of the European Union.

Of course, this shift in power had been going on for some time. National rulers often needed to borrow money from bankers, and this gave bankers considerable influence on policy. Few histories of Europe give adequate attention to the role of banks. The Cold War that took over soon after World War II was partly another war between nations. However, as was often recognized, it was also a war between two economic systems: capitalism and communism. Nothing of that sort had ever occurred before.

The United States did not surrender sovereignty to any community of nations. Nevertheless, it may be a clearer instance of the shift from nationalism to economism than the European nations. It accepted leadership of the "Free World," by which was meant the world that is free from communism. To be in the service of capitalism meant to subordinate national interests, as measured in nonmonetary ways, or even GNP per capita, to effectiveness in pursuing the goals of capitalists. As long as the capitalists in question lived and worked within the nation, one could find some congruence between their interests and the pursuit of national wealth characteristic of nationalism. Nations for some time pursued economic goals primarily as means of strengthening themselves over against other nations.

But the interests of capitalism were to minimize national boundaries, and the great corporations became global in scope. This was especially true of financial institutions. The United States began to serve global industrial corporations and the global banking system, often at the expense of the American people. Trade agreements are designed to limit the power of political agencies in relation to corporations. This has been a dramatic expression of the shift from nationalism to economism.

Americans who are unhappy with this development are told that this is a democracy; so, if they want to return to nationalism, they have only to elect representatives who will do so. To some extent this has taken place in the election of Donald Trump. Much to the distress of the capitalist establishment, Trump has intensified national borders that were being rendered unimportant by the globalization of corporations and "trade agreements." He wants American corporations to serve the American nation.

However, this strengthening of nationalism is not a rejection of economism in general. He serves the world of American wealth, appeasing the rich and their institutions by enriching them at the expense of the rest of the citizenry. He may really believe that in the long run wealth will trickle down. But this is a different form of economism rather than a return to previous forms of nationalism.

He is dismantling those nationalist programs instituted to protect the people from purely economistic treatment. Nationalists typically took pride in the beauty and health of their nation, even in the liberty and political participation of their citizens. Trump's politics are focused on fuller transfer of power to those who think only of immediate financial gain.

For a short time after World War II, American capitalism seemed to be dominated by industrial corporations. But, fairly rapidly, real power shifted from the industrial world to the financial institutions. Of course, much of the time, the interests of industry and finance coincide. Both aim to reduce the power of national governments to restrict business and the flow of capital. But in the "free world," private finance controls the money supply and has a more direct power over politics than does industry.

In the long run, financiers would benefit from intact ecosystems, a world with plenty of topsoil, and oceans that support lots of fish. But they have been schooled by economists who focus only on increasing market activity. Even continuing the present level of economic activity is extremely likely to make the planet uninhabitable. The general increase of economic activity speeds the coming of utter catastrophe. Nothing is more important than to end the actual reign of economism, whether global or nationalistic, and that will not happen unless its domination of popular thinking, as well as scholarly theory, is ended.

☀11☀

DECONSTRUCTING AMERICAN
SELF-UNDERSTANDING

C URRENTLY, the views and actions of the United States have an
exaggerated influence on the history of the world. In addition,
I am writing as a citizen of the United States primarily for other
citizens. Even in the previous chapter, the American perspective
may have been apparent to the reader. But I am adding a chapter
explicitly directed to us. Our deconstructing of our particular
self-understanding is important, not only for us, but also for all
living things.

AMERICAN EXCEPTIONALISM

In the previous chapter, I discussed nationalism, and what I say
there applies to the American case. However, because of the
extreme importance to the planet as a whole of how Americans
think of themselves, I am returning to this topic. Much of what
I say about American exceptionalism can be paralleled in other
countries. It is natural to evaluate all by the standards of your own
culture, and when you do that, you are likely to find that your

culture excels; that in some ways important to you, it is unique, that is, an exception.

I grew up in Japan, and there is no question that there are unique features, some very attractive, of Japanese culture. Further, the view of themselves on the part of the Japanese people at that time tended to divinize their emperor, thus reinforcing their uniqueness. Over millennia, no foreign army had invaded Japan.

Japanese exceptionalism led to the belief that the lot of anyone ruled by the emperor was superior, so that its conquest of Korea and Manchuria and Formosa, were good for the conquered. The great expansion of Japan's empire in the early years of World War II confirmed that the Japanese military was invincible. The willingness of the Japanese to die for the emperor would enable them to defeat any enemy. The commitment of pilots to suicide, *kamikaze,* was an expression of Japanese exceptionalism, one that they thought guaranteed victory. In the end, of course, they were defeated, despite their remarkable attitude and commitment.

Spiritually and culturally the adjustment to the possibility of being conquered was painful and difficult. I am sure that the sense of their own uniqueness has not disappeared, but whatever is left of it takes less dangerous forms. Indeed, Japanese have much be proud of, and pride in positive accomplishments is healthy. Part of Japan's current uniqueness is the intensity with which it supports peace.

Unfortunately, American exceptionalism is more like Japanese exceptionalism before World War II than like current Japanese exceptionalism. Americans tend to think that our goals are beneficial to those we control. The Japanese thought that Koreans benefited from being under the rule of the Japanese emperor. Most Koreans did not agree. We think South Korea is fortunate to be under American military hegemony. Most South Koreans would prefer to be independent, and many would like to reunite with North Korea. We Americans think of the United States as committed to democracy and human rights and as promoting these all around the world. Many people elsewhere have found that the United States overthrows democratically elected governments and that human rights are trashed by dictators imposed by us.

Like the self-image of many countries, there is some truth in ours. The American Declaration of Independence and the American Constitution completed by the first ten amendments, have inspired people all over the world to aim at democracy and human rights. Our success in liberating ourselves from British rule with these goals led to emulation elsewhere. We were not alone in believing ourselves to be in the lead in these matters.

Our view that when we made the decisions for other people, they benefited also had some historical basis. The American occupation of Japan under MacArthur's control was excellent for the Japanese people in many respects. MacArthur broke up the conglomerates that had excessive political and economic power. He broke up large farms and gave ownership to those who had worked them. He got the Japanese to adopt a pacifist constitution. He helped to humanize the emperor without destroying the imperial system. Human rights were emphasized along with democratic governance.

The United States has not always treated immigrants well. Nevertheless, it has done a remarkable job of taking people of many nationalities and creating a unified nation. Religious freedom and cultural diversity are allowed without fragmenting the body politic. Despite the recent restrictions in the name of security, I write critically about my country without fear of punishment. There is much about the United States of which we can be proud; some of it is truly exceptional.

Our problem is much like that of Japan before World War II. Most of the people over whom the Japanese extended the emperor's beneficent rule were opposed to it, but the Japanese did not understand this. We are so sure of our virtue, and of the benefits we bestow on others, that we are blind to much of the legitimate anger that we arouse among our dependents. We spend more on our military than the rest of the nations combined, and so we consider ourselves invincible. We do not notice that we are already losing ground. Even though we know that we have troops all over the world, we do not consider ourselves an imperial power.

The history of our country that we learn in school is essentially celebratory, so we simply do not notice the dark side of our history and of our current policies. Our blindness is recognized by people all over the world. They know that if any other countries acted as we act, we would consider it inexcusable and see to it that they were severely sanctioned. Consider, for example, how we would react if Russia engaged in drone warfare in Mexico. It would confirm all of our worst projections. But because it is we who are doing it, and because we know that our motives are pure and our actions are for the sake of people everywhere, we support, or at least tolerate, our own practice. We are not told how the countries where we kill people in this way feel about this mode of killing their citizens, and, derivatively, how they feel about us.

Nations that do not recognize the evil they do in the eyes of the world are not making themselves more secure. We need to free ourselves from erroneous or one-sided understandings of our history and current actions. Only a people who know who they really have been and are can be trusted to lead the world wisely.

So, who are we? What happened in our history that we ignore? This is a large topic. I will mention only a few points. First, from the arrival of the first settlers until today we have been in constant imperial expansion. One of the crimes of which we accused the British government, justifying our revolt, was its effort to protect the indigenous people from our genocidal advance. Once we rid ourselves of British rule, that advance continued, and it has not ceased, even today.

Second, our country's economy was built to a large extent on slave labor. Of course, everyone knows that slavery is a blot on our record, but our emphasis in recalling our history is that we freed the slaves. They, and the continued exploitation and segregation of African Americans, tend to drop from history until Martin Luther King again forced attention. Once more, the history we live by emphasizes that we ended segregation.

Third, a major part of our foreign policy dealt with Latin America. While we celebrate the extension of our great nation from sea to shining sea, we pay little attention, not only to the genocide of indigenous people but to the theft of land from Mexico. Meanwhile, our "Monroe doctrine" may have helped some Latin American countries gain independence from Europe, but it sucked them into our orbit of economic exploitation. The most decorated soldier in the U.S. Army, General Smedley Darlington Butler, after frequent battles in Latin America, finally understood that all the killing and dying of the soldiers he led into battle was for the sake of U.S. corporate profits. In 1935, he wrote *War is a Racket* and devoted the rest of his life to sharing this understanding with the American people. Regrettably, the truth he exposed has not found its way into our collective memory. Sadly, few Americans even know of this true American hero.

Fourth, In Latin America, we have frequently destroyed democratic governments in favor of military regimes that took orders from us. This is continuing to happen today around the world. In my youth, I rejoiced that I was not a citizen of one of those bad European colonial powers. The truth, of course, is that our overall record is one of the worst. It provides no basis for others to trust our intentions. When we realize that our military operations today are in the service of corporations, now especially international financial corporations, we have every reason to withdraw support from established U.S. policy. It is time to recognize that we are one nation among others, with our strengths and weaknesses, but with no mandate to rule the world.

AMERICAN DEFENSE

One adage that is used to cover a great many absurdities is that the best defense is a good offense. All individuals and all nations are viewed as justified in defending themselves against the attack of others. What kinds of actions are allowable or desirable in that defense is a matter of discussion. A few call for only nonviolent defense. This may mean that an individual accepts serious injury or death rather than injure or kill another person. But there have been instances when skillful use of nonviolent defense has accomplished a great deal more than the use of violence against a far more powerful adversary.

We Americans, however, can assume that our Department of Defense is not discussing such matters. All evidence points to the primary interest in extending military and political control over the entire planet, what is called "full sector dominance." In short, we act as if the only, or at least, the best, way to "defend" ourselves is to attack and control everyone who does not serve us, which means, as explained above, anyone who does not serve the Western financial system.

In order for Americans to be willing to be heavily taxed to support this imperialist enterprise, they must be persuaded that it is indeed financed for the sake of the security of American lives and property. That is what the word "defense" is ordinarily supposed to mean. Accordingly, almost any sum of money can be demanded for "defense," with little or no opposition in Congress. To be accused of being soft on defense is assumed to be the kiss of death, politically speaking. Few things are more important for reducing our destruction of the life system on the planet than redirecting the expenditures of the American government from global imperialism to the well-being of people, especially, of course, the American people—and the natural world. Understanding that our expenditures for "defense" actually make our lives and well-being more precarious could be a first step toward the exercise of common sense.

The deceptive use of "defense" goes farther. Thus far, it has prevented auditing the Department of Defense. It is highly probable that large sums are siphoned off to enrich the rich, and that defense contracts are not entirely directed to serving military needs efficiently. In short, powerful people have much to conceal. An item in OpEdNews.com (July 4, 2018) asserts that the 2015 Report of the (DoD) Inspector General states that there was $6.5 trillion of unaccounted-for Pentagon spending that year. Suspicion is heightened even more by a remarkable feature of the 9/11 attack on the Pentagon. The part of the Pentagon at which it was directed was the section where financial records were kept. Congress had finally decided on an audit, which then became impossible.

I have focused on the Department of Defense. The situation is similar with the FBI and the CIA. These two are supposed to be defending us. They, together with the Congress that funds them so generously, think that we are enemies of our own defense and so must be carefully reined in. The freedoms of which we brag are being taken from us in the name of security.

If half of the resources now provided to the "security establishment" were spent on working for peace, justice, and prosperity along with improving global ecosystems, there might be a chance for the healthy survival of civilization. But currently there is no discussion of any reduction in what we spend on "defense" and "security," or any assessment of its actual achievements. "Defense" and "security" sound great. So, we throw more money at them, guaranteeing widespread loss and suffering.

THE AMERICAN UNIVERSITY

The discussion of American exceptionalism suggests that a standard American education gives a dangerously one-sided picture of American history. We understand that this is almost inevitable. A major function of schooling has been to turn immigrants from many nations and cultures into American citizens. All history writing is selective. To write a text book on American history for such a purpose will always lead to selections favorable to American self-appreciation. But we comfort ourselves by supposing that the American leaders of the future will go on to college and there acquire more accurate knowledge.

As with so many widely held suppositions, there is some truth to this. In a college or university history department, there will be a number of courses going into great detail on some segment of American history. If one majors in American history and takes many of these courses, one will certainly understand that the popular view is seriously mistaken. But, it is unlikely that the department will help much in developing an alternative overview. In history departments of contemporary universities, the goal is not to develop comprehensive views of what has occurred and its meaning for orienting us today. It is to acquire accurate factual information about particular events. This tends to leave the historical basis for American exceptionalism little changed, even for many specialists. And, of course, the percentage of students who specialize in American history is very small.

I begin with this as an example of how American universities do not fulfill the expectations that many outsiders hold for them. Since these expectations are of important human functions, until we recognize that universities are about something else, we will leave these functions unfulfilled. There are some things that modern universities do well. They should be congratulated and appreciated. But meeting the world's, or the nation's, greatest needs is not among them.

If we are to save the world, either universities must change, or we must find other ways of educating. This is recognized by the title—*Save the World on Your Own Time*—of a book written by Stanley Fish, a famous educator, to university professors. He makes it clear that universities hire professors to do research on limited topics. They then are to pass on those methods and the information gained to their students.

Our greatest universities call themselves "value-free research universities." Being free of values means in part being free of prejudices and open to the evidence. That is admirable. But it also means that values are considered unimportant, and this judgment of unimportance is transmitted to students. This makes the "modern university," a type that became normative only after World War II, unique in the history of education, which has heretofore always been about values. "Saving the world" is a value. I think it is a very important value that should inform our whole educational system. But because it is a value, discussion of this possibility is excluded from the most prestigious modern American universities.

The incentive for attending a university today is usually the expectation of improving job prospects, judged by salaries, that is, by money. Although the intention of the university is to serve the rapid increase of known facts, which facts are made known, and even how they are formulated, tends to be determined by money. Unfortunately, the research for which money is available is more likely to serve the profits of corporations than the sustainability of human life.

In the preceding chapter I criticized the dominant metaphysics and the worldview with which modern science has allied itself. I claimed that the evidence gained by scientific research called for revision of the metaphysics that still shapes most science. Universities were once places where questions about assumptions could be asked. They were, in other words, places supportive of intellectual activity. Today they are not. If intellectual reflection were encouraged, I feel quite sure that the commitment to a seventeenth-century philosophy would give way. That could open the door to an interest in wisdom that could provide helpful guidance about the pressing issues of personal, social, and national life. I am confident that the current threats to human life would be recognized and that our educational system would be reconceived to help us, rather than to block interest in the most important questions.

⚛12⚛

HOW ECOLOGICAL
CIVILIZATION IS POSSIBLE

CHAPTERS TEN AND ELEVEN have sketched widespread assumptions and features of thought that work against the changes so urgently needed. Of course, they do not characterize everyone. Fortunately, criticism of most of these assumptions abounds. But I fear that they still have a hold on many of us, sometimes quite unconscious, that makes serious consideration of needed changes difficult. Perhaps identifying and articulating these assumptions will help to loosen their hold.

The more we emphasize the need for changing our minds, that is, for what the New Testament calls "repentance," the more radical we depict that change as being, the more we invite the criticism that this is all idle wishing. It is "utopian" in the bad sense of having no possible place in the real world. We are wasting our time.

We are not helped in response by having to acknowledge that Jesus failed in what he understood to be his chief mission. The people of Israel, as a whole, did not change in the way he thought required to prevent the destruction of Israel. They suffered the fate Jesus anticipated but hoped to prevent. If we are Jesus's disciples, why should we suppose that we might fare better?

My answer is that although Jesus failed, he also changed history. Obviously, the most visible change was to spawn a church with more members than any other religious community. No one would deny that his followers have played important roles in European history, and, indeed, in the history of the world.

Sadly, the roles of Jesus's followers have been very ambiguous. Murders and slaughters have taken place in his name. In some periods, Christian history has been told in a celebratory way, but today the unveiling of its evil aspects has gone so far that the good that was done in Jesus's name is sometimes forgotten. In this chapter, where we are trying to justify hope, we will focus on positive effects, but there is no intention to deny the genocides, sexual exploitation of children, and other horrors that equally characterize the history of the church. Unless we truly repent, there is no hope, and repentance requires facing the worst without defensiveness.

I suggest that when we ask what is possible, we approach the goal in three steps. First, is it possible that the nations of the world would follow China in declaring that an "ecological civilization" is their shared goal? For us to consider this accomplished, the language would not have to be just these words. Pope Francis's call for "integral ecology," as explained in *Laudato Si*, would be an excellent alternative. Or perhaps disciples of Jesus might want to use his language and call for a "divine commonwealth," spelling that out in a way appropriate to our time. Some might simply return to the language of the 1970s and call for a "sustainable society." Others have suggested replacing "sustainable" by "regenerative."

The choice of language has importance, but the fundamental question is whether the commitment expressed thereby has the essential features of what we are calling "ecological civilization." These include an appreciation for humanity being an integral part of a natural world, in which everything is interconnected and interdependent. It is necessary that the distinctive role of human beings in this interconnected world be recognized, and that humans be called to commit themselves to the well-being of the whole. This entails that every sector of society be restructured so as to serve this integrated whole. It obviously requires the immediate rejection of war as an instrument of international policy.

The first step toward an ecological civilization, to the actualization of that to which we are committed, is, under whatever name, for the nations of the world to reorder their lives for peace. The United States must lead. This would be a radical reversal of American policy.

The second step is to actualize whatever the people already agree about, while devoting significant resources to clarifying what further steps are required and possible. Individual countries may be able to take the lead on major changes and inspire others. Local experiments of all kinds should be encouraged. Educational institutions should become centers of thought and experiment. Religious communities should help people understand the change as expressive of their commitments. Moving too hastily on some fronts might do more harm than good. But delaying action and reflection are certain to worsen the now inevitable disasters toward which we are rushing.

The third step is to survey globally all that is being done, and to plan for global implementation of the best programs, policies, and procedures across the board. These will be designed collectively to actualize ecological civilization. This includes policies and procedures in agriculture, in education, in the legal system, in international affairs, in religious teaching, etc., etc. Most important of all is the implementation of an economy that supports ecological civilization.

There must be a fourth step. Even when a civilization organizes itself in an ecological way, it will continue to have many problems. We are not expecting an idyllic world where everyone gets along with everyone else and all are blissful all the time. We are hoping for a world so organized that it is no longer bent toward self-destruction—a world that encourages frugality rather than waste, and cooperation more than competition. We aim at a world that will understand progress as movement in the direction of improving prospects for future flourishing.

This is the world we disciples of Jesus will understand to be the "divine commonwealth" for our time. I believe that precisely because some of Jesus's ideas have become effective in society, chiefly in the twentieth century, then to aim at actualizing this world is to become part of a movement that has a chance of success. This chapter describes some of the changes that have taken place in recent history that contribute to making the actualization of ecological civilization possible.

I will begin with changes in the church that claims to recognize Jesus as Lord and Savior. One major change has been its great decline in Europe and North America. But as my focus here is on changes that support the movement toward ecological civilization. I will focus on Protestantism in the United States.

In the first half of the nineteenth century, Protestantism in this country was fragmented. Each denomination had its distinctive characteristics and tended to accent them in opposition to others. For the most part, they understood their ultimate role as assisting people to prepare for the final judgment of each individual. Some put more emphasis on right beliefs; some, on right behavior. Some had a deeper understanding of the meaning of "faith." But the wider context tended to be common.

Although this individualistic Christianity was dominant, I explained earlier that the Social Gospel, which arose in response, has the basic commitment to social and personal transformation that is required today for ecological civilization. It was not a minor factor in the churches. Officially it had the support of whole denominations. There is no longer any doubt that Christians can organize in large numbers in a struggle to improve society as a whole.

When Martin Luther King persuaded white practitioners to include racial justice in their social gospel and then went on to add peace and the ending of poverty, much of what constitutes an ecological civilization was already convincingly proposed. To move forward from there to the call for ecological civilization is not so big a leap. Millions of believers have already made these moves.

The focus on making a difference in society and in the larger biosphere led denominations to shift from rivalry to cooperation. The "ecumenical movement" was initially a move toward unity among these denominations. The National Council of Churches developed shared guidelines about the changes for which the denominations should all work. This was something of a blueprint for Franklin Roosevelt's New Deal.

Protestant churches also organized globally in the World Council of Churches, partnering with Eastern Orthodox Churches. The discussions in the WCC were enriched by the perspectives of Africans, Asians, and Latin Americans. In the second half of the twentieth century, the global church addressed global problems with some sophistication. Asking the churches through established channels to contribute to ecological civilization has become an easy next step.

Meanwhile, the impulse of denominations toward cooperation with one another was extended to other Abrahamic traditions and then to those of south and east Asia. The Parliament of World Religions meeting in Chicago at the outset of the twentieth century awakened many American Protestants to the fact that much of value and importance was to be found in traditions that had previously been viewed with condescension. This new understanding has moved from the margins to the mainstream. The teaching of world religions in colleges has become standard. Religious exclusivism has changed from being taken for granted to being something to be avoided.

I have focused on North American Protestantism. Global Roman Catholicism has moved more cautiously and perhaps more skillfully through similar changes. Its social teachings have been important especially in Catholic countries but also in the labor movement in the United States.

It was more difficult for the Roman Catholic Church to acknowledge the full Christianity of Protestant churches, but at Vatican II it largely overcame its own exclusivism both toward other Christians and toward other faith communities. And in *Laudato Si*, the Pope has addressed the whole of humanity in a call for something very like ecological civilization.

There remain many negatives. Conservative Protestants feel that those who have moved to a social gospel and ecumenical and interfaith activities have abandoned their Christian faith. Many Catholic leaders drag their feet with regard to the pope's present initiative. Not all Muslims, Jews, Hindus, and Buddhists care to respond to Christian initiatives for cooperation. The religious world is still fragmented and contentious.

But much leadership in all traditions favors working together to solve the world's practical problems. This is quite different from the situation faced by Jesus, and his teaching has played a role in effecting the change. The opposition in religious communities to further moves toward ecological civilization is, in fact, fragmented and weak.

Central to Jesus's teaching is God's universal, unconditional love. We are to love one another in a similar way. This has one consequence that has not been brought out as clearly in other traditions. We are to love our enemies.

From this principle we cannot directly deduce complete nonviolence. Jesus is depicted as having used some violence against the money changers in the temple. One can argue that parents may sometimes use physical force in punishing their children precisely out of love. If one loves both the victim of violence and the one who is inflicting it, violent intervention to stop the violence may express love for all. I do not think that Jesus taught nonviolence universally and absolutely.

What he did teach was more radical than the usual formulations of nonviolent resistance. Going the second mile is a positive expression of love directed to the oppressor. Since love of the oppressor is clearly taught, we may say that this expression of love flows naturally without regard for consequences. But Paul noted that the result would be heaping hot coals on the head of the oppressor. It may well be that Jesus taught doing good to the oppressor because one loved him. But he also believed that expressing love in this way would disrupt the system of oppression.

Seeking practical advice from Jesus about how to deal with oppressors did not occur, as far as I know, before the Hindu, Gandhi. Gandhi derived the ideal of loving the enemy from Jesus, and he integrated it with nonviolent resistance. His goal was, like that of Jesus, to express love even for enemies. Jesus believed that by ignoring normal rules based on standard rights and duties, and by abandoning all attachment to being treated justly, one could end the structures of oppression that work through this pattern. Gandhi focused on mass demonstrations that affirmed the British as human beings, but also forced them to recognize that the Indians were also human beings who should be respected. It was probably the only tactic that would have won independence at that time. In other words, the first time anyone followed this part of Jesus's teaching on the world stage, the approach worked. Jesus had no preceding success to point to. We have.

Jesus's teaching also played a role in another remarkable experiment in the twentieth century. In South Africa, when white rule was nonviolently ended, a Truth and Reconciliation Committee was established. South African Christians understood that the deep grievances of exploited and immiserated blacks could not be simply ignored. Without their forgiveness of the whites, South Africa's political future was dark. But they could not be asked to forgive whites of crimes that whites did not even acknowledge. First truth, then reconciliation. It was effective. Again, obviously, it was not perfect. But it stands as a real historical possibility that can function for other nations as well.

We can say with assurance that Gandhi's success is not treated today as a fluke. It has been a model for action in many places. The most important was Martin Luther King's transformation of laws and attitudes about race by the tactic of expressing love for all, including the oppressors—while resisting nonviolently.

The change effected by King was truly remarkable. It was not just a change of laws in the United States. Similar changes occurred globally. King's work transformed the understanding of racism. Before King, almost everyone was a "racist" in at least some respects. Most people saw no reason to deny their racism. Today, no one wants to be labelled in that way, least of all those who are, in fact, most obviously racist. This global reversal required only a generation.

It is clear that Jesus's teaching is congenial to the ending of racism. In his day, people were largely defined by their ethnicity. There were Jews and Gentiles, Greeks and barbarians. Geographically, in Israel, there were Jews and Samaritans. Jesus accepted these distinctions, but his actions and his teachings worked against drawing from them the typical conclusions. All are children of God and proper objects of our love.

The gospels record Jesus as straining his relations with leaders of his own community by telling stories that indicated people from despised ethnic backgrounds were often better. A Samaritan is the hero of one of his most famous parables. When Gentiles listened and believed, he celebrated this and commented on their superiority to many Jews in this respect.

Paul made explicit what was implicit in Jesus's teaching and actions. As long as Jesus's mission was to save the Jews from self-destruction, the distinction between Jews and Gentiles played some role. After his death, that mission ended. The communities that grew up around him and his memory focused on embodying the divine commonwealth. For this purpose, the lines between Jews and Gentiles and between Greeks and barbarians were erased. The distinction of Black and White played no role in early Christianity. East Asians were not involved. And Jesus made no general pronouncements against racism.

It is painfully obvious that, in later periods, racial distinctions, prejudice, oppression, enslavement, and even genocide have received support of various sorts from some who claimed to be Christian. In Paul's day, slavery was not primarily connected to race. Hence, for him, it was important to affirm as a separate matter that in Christ there is no slave or free. Sadly, movements against racism and slavery were opposed by many in the churches. My own ancestors were pious Christian slaveholders.

It would be too much to say that ending the public acceptance of racism was a result of Jesus's ministry. Nevertheless, Jesus and the early church were as free from racism as was possible at that time. In later centuries, from time to time, Jesus's teaching inspired some disciples to work against particularly brutal expressions of racism, such as slavery. If we trace the history, we cannot ignore the role of Jesus in the opposition to racism. And through the work of Martin Luther King, we find that the use of Jesus's methods accomplished, on a global scale, a goal implicit in Jesus's teaching and practice.

I am not suggesting that racism has ceased to be a powerful force in the United States, one that poisons much of life for many people. The collective decision that racism is an evil, one that society must oppose, has not cleansed the feelings and thoughts of everyone or even of most people. Adoption of the goal of ecological civilization by nations, churches, corporations, and schools will not end the selfishness that leads to frequent and repeated violations of what is needed.

But, today, public debates are about how to combat racism, not about whether it is acceptable. And real progress has been made. Although Trump's leadership has made racist statements and practices almost respectable, few want the term "racist" applied to them. It is unlikely that our society will revert to its previous avowed and legalized racism. Progress on this front is at the same time a move toward ecological civilization. When public debates about the economy are about how to end excessive use of nature's bounty, we will have taken another step.

Another front on which Paul anticipated major progress that has occurred in our time is feminism. He made the startling statement that in Christ there is neither male nor female. One cannot find a comparable statement in Jesus, but women played an unusually important role in his movement. Some were clearly his friends, such as Mary and Martha, the sisters of Lazarus. Mary Magdalene is the last follower with the crucified Jesus and the first with the resurrected one. She is depicted as sufficiently close to Jesus to be credited with a gospel, and her relationship with Jesus is the object of much speculation.

Many of those who were healed were women, and it was their faith to which Jesus attributed the healing. The women were the first to discover that Jesus was resurrected. No disparaging remarks about women are reported in the gospels. Women were leaders in Paul's churches.

Sadly, patriarchal attitudes quickly asserted themselves in the new churches. They were even inserted into Paul's letters. The church became a bastion of patriarchy. To this day the Roman Catholic Church has been unable to liberate itself. I dare to say that some women through the centuries, and especially in recent times, have been strengthened in their resolve to demand justice by the assurance of support from Jesus and Paul. But we Christians must admit that the remarkable achievements of the modern feminist movement developed outside the churches. That in no way takes away from the claim that the success of the feminist movement paves the way for ecological civilization.

When we ask about the possibilities of a more radical move toward an ecological civilization, we should note that if King had not been assassinated, there would have been a test. King is best known for his remarkably successful nonviolent work against racism. But he believed more was possible and, indeed, needed, even to secure and deepen the success.

King understood that much of black suffering resulted from black poverty. He knew that much prejudice against blacks came from those whites who also suffer from poverty. He understood that in fact these whites and blacks shared needs and prospects. Some of the elite had long profited financially and politically by pitting "white trash" and "niggers" against one another. Both would benefit once they joined together. King promoted a poor people's march on Washington. He planned to camp on the mall until Congress took real steps to improve the lot of the American poor.

King's vision was still more holistic. He understood that anti-Communism and the wars it generated were an important part of the system that sacrificed the poor and kept them poor. The resources devoted to war could, if redirected, go far toward solving the problems of the poor. The march demanded the end of the Vietnam War and a major change of budgets away from the armed forces.

Was there a possibility of success? Perhaps not. But the most plausible explanation of his assassination is that the establishment was deeply concerned about this threat. This is the view of the King family, and it was supported in a public trial in Memphis. It would be naïve to deny that the established order was in real danger. The threat was that the United States government would take a major step toward an ecological civilization and bring about a system that the powers that be could not control. That there was such a possibility, then, says to me that in working for an ecological civilization we are not merely fantasizing about something that has always been impossible.

The ending of the imperial venture of the United States would have opened up possibilities around the world. Those who support American hegemony often claim that nations have always warred with one another and that the result would be worse than the Pax Americana that now exists. This raises another question about the current prospect of peace that is an indispensable part of any ecological civilization. Is there an alternative to endless wars among nations? More that once in preceding chapters I have pointed to the European Union as indicating that it is possible to organize internationally in a way that makes war among the participating nations unthinkable.

Again, the European Union is far from perfect. Some countries have been exploited and oppressed within the union, especially by its financial instruments. Europe, as a whole, has participated in wars. The European Union is having major problems. But if, in the world as a whole, war became as unlikely to break out as it now is among the nations belonging to the European Union, I would declare success in this area in becoming an ecological civilization.

Without making specific claims about Jesus's teaching, we can say that war has always been difficult to reconcile with Christian faith and practice, and that Jesus's influence did play a role in the formation of the European Union. The key players in creating the European Union, De Gaulle of France and Adenauer of Germany, considered themselves to be Christians.

I have gone to some trouble to indicate that Jesus's influence played a role in recent developments that suggest the goal of ecological civilization is possible. We disciples of Jesus could celebrate these developments regardless of any connection of this kind, but because the connection factually exists, and because we rejoice in any role Jesus has played in a saving way in our history, these asides are worthwhile. Jesus failed to prevent the destruction of Israel by Rome. But he is not "a failure." To be his disciple does not entail any assurance of success. But we are not throwing our lives away on a "loser."

Sometimes there are ways in which what I consider the acts of our enemies work in our favor. This may be true with respect to war. Although we have had many wars in the process of building the American empire, the most fearsome weapon in our arsenal has not been used again after World War II. Also, despite deep enmity between the United States and the Soviet Union, there was no war. In that case, it is highly probable that what prevented war was "mutually assured destruction."

Nations have fought many wars for stupid reasons or none. But perhaps the near certainty that you will be killed in the war, and your nation laid waste, does deter nations from crossing certain lines. Today, we have to hope that in relation to Korea the amount of damage that North Korea can inflict on us and our allies is sufficient to deter an attack and even encourage work for peace. However, even though we welcome all allies in preventing war, it is obvious that an ever-accelerating race to see how one nation can destroy another without being destroyed is not the peace that reliably contributes to ecological civilization.

I hope I have made it clear that there have been changes in recent times, partly as a result of Jesus's influence, that have generated deep resonance to the call to implement something like the divine commonwealth today. This project cannot be easily dismissed as merely utopian. On the other hand, in my argument against impossibility, I may have given too optimistic a picture.

The forces arrayed against us are immensely powerful, so powerful that the only member of our team whom they took seriously was King. He was a threat, and the establishment knows what to do with those who really threaten it. The forces that constitute the "deep state," or what I am calling "the establishment," are primarily economic institutions, teachings, and practices. These are important opponents in themselves, but they also control our political institutions, the military and security establishments, the media, the educational system, our agriculture, and much else. In these areas, any influence of Jesus is hard to discern.

As of now, there are no large movements oriented to achieving something like ecological civilization. However, even here we can find glimmers of hope. Trump's election awakened many Americans to the need to involve themselves in politics. Usually the involvement is narrowly focused, but the youth awakened by shootings in schools gave encouraging breadth to their demands. Perhaps the younger generation of voting age people will be drawn into politics, and perhaps this will bring to the issues a wider and more urgent call for change. There have been proposals for them to break with the current two-party system, about which they are rightly cynical, and establish a third party not beholden to Wall Street or oil companies.

In one way or another a party representing the people rather than the corporate world may emerge. If that occurs, real change is possible. We do not have a scenario, but that is no reason not to hope and try.

If out of the current ferment, a movement emerges whose leadership is dispersed, assassination will not prove an effective weapon to destroy it. Control of the major media will not determine the thinking of younger Americans who understand that these media cannot be trusted. Even leaders in academia have limited authority with them. Still, they may achieve enough consensus for effective action. We can hope.

This book is written for the American public and particularly for any who may join me in the effort to be disciples of Jesus. Most of my previous reflection about the prospects of ecological civilization have been with the Chinese, who have already taken the first step of making it an explicit and comprehensive goal. They are engaged in what I called early in this chapter the second step. They are not very active in pursuing the many dimensions that need to be acted on and rethought, but they are far ahead of the rest of us. I have earlier reported that the Chinese decision to develop the villages in the countryside rather than tear them down for the sake of industrial agriculture has led to a significant revival of life in rural areas.

In addition, growth goals in China are set below levels that could be reached so that attention can be paid to the environmental effects of economic policies. Governors are evaluated both by the growth they supervise and by the health of the environment. Efforts to close coal mines and get energy from the sun continue alongside of work to eliminate what the United Nations labels as "poverty."

And, finally, can any of the developments in China be seen as influenced by Jesus? Direct influence of Jesus is unlikely to have been important, but, the influence of Marx is pervasive. Marx was influenced by the same tradition that influenced Jesus, the Hebrew prophets. We who try to be disciples of Jesus are cousins of those who share the Marxist legacy. The Chinese Marxists have accepted the participation of their Christian cousins in advancing the ecological civilization to which they have committed themselves.

✴13✴

CAN GOD HELP?

I F WE FOLLOWED what is considered "orthodox" Christian theology instead of Jesus, this would be a silly question. In that theology, it is asserted that God can do anything. Presumably, God could cause the whole world to achieve a perfect form of ecological civilization at any moment. In that case, we could beseech God to do that. Or we could decide that since God has not created an ecological civilization, God does not want it, and we should therefore decide not to seek it. Or, since God has complete control over our decisions as well, we could just leave it all up to God. One could draw the conclusion that concerning ourselves about what happens, when, in fact God controls it all, is silly. Indeed, if God has all the power, then God is already doing everything that is done. We might wonder why God is causing all this charade of confusing ideas in our minds, but we would also know that there was nothing for us to do about it.

Actually, taking the doctrine of divine omnipotence rigorously leads to a way of understanding what happens in the world that is both remote from common sense and remote from the biblical texts. If God has all the power, then there cannot even be resistance to God. We are in no way responsible for what we do. The worst sins are all God's doings. This is very different from Jesus's Abba.

In reaction to the absurdities that result from believing that there is an omnipotent God, moderns have decided that it is matter that is omnipotent. Everything that happens consists in nothing but bits of matter in motion and can be completely explained by antecedent movements of bits of matter. In one sense, this seems to be the opposite doctrine to divine omnipotence. God does nothing, matter does everything. But the effects with respect to ourselves are much the same. Our attempts to act turn out to be completely pointless. The turmoil of confused ideas in our minds is the result of matter in motion. So, of course, is our belief that everything is matter in motion. Beliefs so caused might happen to be true, but that seems very unlikely, since matter has no interest in truth.

I go through this little exercise in hopes that we can all agree to reject any simple-minded reductionism that undercuts all reasons for asking questions. Let's ask for explanations and be open to diversity. Let's not rule out all sorts of causes in advance. Let's suppose that much of the world consists in matter in motion and is explained by other matter in motion. Let us suppose that some things are explained by human decisions. And let us stay open to the possibility that some things are explained by God. If such diversity exists, then questioning what we can do, and what God can do, makes sense.

The modern university basically follows the matter-in-motion model, which it derives from the Cartesian view of nature. Of course, the unversity does not explicitly draw all the nihilistic implications. The student gets the impression that she or he has some responsibility for behavior and that one *should* not cheat on exams. But the university provides no explanation for this value judgment, and as a value-free institution, it explicitly dismisses its importance. Perhaps there is nothing wrong with cheating if one can get away with it.

One way of identifying the role of God is to ask what phenomena, that we consider important, are excluded from the world consisting of matter in motion. We can begin with purpose, since Descartes's exclusion of purpose from nature is emphatic and explicit. My previous formulations indicate that since the Cartesian dualism that left the soul as a purposing entity is now rejected, personal responsibility is also excluded. This would require freedom and/or self-determination for which the world of matter in motion has no place. And since everything is fully explained by what already exists or has happened, radical novelty cannot occur.

Now, few people in their practical lives completely deny or ignore this family of experiences. In general, the university, like the family and the public life, functions as if people had purposes and were responsible for what they did. But the university has faith that ultimately it will be shown that this is not really the case; so, ideas of purpose and responsibility must be kept out of the classroom while assumed in the dormitory. This follows the model of Immanuel Kant, the most influential philosopher of the nineteenth century, who sharply distinguished the "theoretical reason" of the classroom and the "practical reason" of the dormitory.

However, we find that the decision that purpose and responsibility cannot be accepted as part of the theoretical world is based on a seventeenth-century metaphysics that is rarely discussed in the university and fits poorly with contemporary science. Surely its authority can be questioned. This metaphysics excludes God, *a priori*, from a theoretical or explanatory role. If instead we decide to develop a way of thinking based on experience, we may end up in a quite different place.

My suggestion is that we take all our experience as real and begin by explaining as much of it as we can in a strictly physical way. Modern natural science has learned a great deal in this way.

But rather than saying that the aspects of experience that do not lend themselves to explanation in purely physical terms do not exist, we will introduce a different cause. A great deal of what happens in each moment of my experience is fully explained by past experiences and new events in the brain's neurons. But radical novelty occurs; purposes are real; there is an element of self-determination in human experience. In short, although most of a moment of human experience is the predetermined product of the past, in part it is creatively self-organizing.

Alfred North Whitehead offers a detailed account of the coming into being of a moment of human experience in these terms. Whereas Descartes denies any role for purpose in nature, Whitehead locates human experiences in nature and recognizes that these are purposefully self-organizing. There is an aim at actualizing what value can be actualized in each specific locus, that is, where the past is just what it is. No part of that past can be completely ignored, but just what role it plays may be affected by the way it is synthesized. Also, this synthesizing may require the introduction of possibilities not derived from that past.

We now know that we are natural animals with close relatives in other animal species. Rather than assume that purpose and self-organization are uniquely human, it makes far more sense to study other species open-mindedly to determine whether there is evidence of purpose and self-organization in them, as well. The finding is that this is by far the most natural way to interpret the data. Indeed, wherever we find life, even among bacteria, the evidence lends itself to such understanding. Today, even quantum events seem better understood on the analogy of human experience than as instances of matter-in-motion.

Much of what the occasion of human experience becomes can be predicted from its past. But the decision about just how to actualize itself is determined only as it occurs. There is much in what a baby is for which she or he is not responsible. But, even by the age of two, the cumulation of decisions made by the infant participate in shaping her or his character. As time passes, a child becomes more and more responsible for what she or he does. The insistence that only what can be physically explained is real, that purposive decisions count for nothing, does not accord with experience.

I started out to talk about God, and I have talked only about human self-determination. Many of those who, like me, greatly appreciate the work of Whitehead in giving us a more credible and inclusive account of experience, stop at this point, but Whitehead does not. We noted that each new momentary experience is initiated by an aim to achieve what value can be achieved then and there. For Whitehead, and for me, this calls for a further explanation. If this happens always and everywhere, it seems to be derivative from a cosmic aim at realizing value.

Whitehead theorizes that the sphere of potentiality, that is, of what may become, is ordered for the sake of realizing value. Recent science has found that the order of the universe contains many features required for the emergence of life but arbitrary from a purely materialist perspective. Whitehead calls this sphere of ordered potential the primordial nature of God. It is because of God that natural occurrences are not simply part of a machine, even though the mechanical model explains much about them. Living things include more than the mechanistic features on which science has focused attention.

Whitehead speculates that God not only affects all events, but that God is also affected by all events. All other entities are involved in both relationships., and he thinks that some forms of religious experience provide evidence for this interaction between God and the world. This corresponds with the way God was thought of in Israel. Jesus's Abba interacts with the world in this way. We who would be Jesus's disciples may quite reasonably follow in this path. It can give us guidance as to what we can reasonably expect of God and how we can work with God for the salvation of the world.

When we shift from the cosmological to the existential perspective, we can identify in ourselves what I name the "call forward." I find that in myself, and I have been pleased to find that
one of the twentieth century's greatest phenomenologists, Martin
Heidegger, found that this characterized his experience as well. I
follow Whitehead in thinking that this call comes, moment by
moment, from God's ordering of the sphere of potentiality and is
thereby directed to the actualization of the greatest good possible
then and there. If so, then cultivating sensitivity to the call and
responding fully to it can be my ideal. What is possible in the next
moment, the form the call takes then, depends on my response in
this moment. I believe this is an interpretation of the call that fits
the experience well.

However, in our day, there is great resistance to introducing
God. Heidegger, as an atheist, could not. For him the call had to
come from the one who is called. In English this self-enclosedness
of experience is translated as "authenticity," making it seem
quite attractive. The German word *eigentlichkeit* makes the self-
enclosedness more explicit. This extreme emphasis on the autonomy
of the individual may have contributed to Heidegger's decision to
support the Nazis. I do not mean to prove the existence of God
by such comments. But it seems to me worthwhile to note the cost
of denying that there is any reality above and beyond our own.

Whitehead's account indicates a very important role of God
in a discipleship to Jesus aiming to bring to realization in current
terms the divine commonwealth he proclaimed. Our actions need
not be wholly governed by our knowledge and reflection. Although
we are often called to study and reflect, and what God can call us
to do is deeply affected by what we learn, a wisdom can work in
us that is not entirely our own.

Jesus told us that where two or three gather in his name, he is in
our midst. In the early church people experienced a spirit when they
gathered that they sometimes thought of as the presence of Jesus

and sometimes as God. Paul also writes of how Wisdom works in and with us. The sense of God's presence and of an empowerment and a guidance that comes with it is a profound part of Christian spiritual experience. Most of this is our experience of the ordered potentiality that Whitehead calls the primordial nature of God, and that participates in every moment of our experience. From God we derive the aim at realizing value, which is so foundational to all our experience.

But this does not exhaust the experience of God. Many have experienced a moment of being totally accepted as they are. For those who have experienced this vividly, there is confidence that, just as God affects us, so also, all we become affects God. The experience is one of compassionate acceptance of all that we are, just as we are. This corresponds with Jesus's teaching about God, whom he called Abba. The God who calls us forgives us even when we refuse the call.

One valid criticism of many advocates of the Social Gospel was that they talked too much about our building the Kingdom of God. We could easily make the same mistake with respect to the divine commonwealth understood as ecological civilization. When we understand God's role in our experience, we know that God is the primary builder. The task of bringing the divine common-wealth is not fundamentally ours. But God works in and through creatures, especially human ones, to that end. Our task is to let God work in and through us. The question to ask should be, not whether God can help us, but whether we can help God.

When I was a youth we used to sing that God has no hands but our hands, and no feet but our feet. In God's own way, God is very powerful. But God's power is radically different from what the word "power" usually connotes in human discourse. God has the power to empower us. All our power to do good derives from God. But God could not pick up the man left beaten by the roadside. It took a Samaritan. God cannot make speeches about ecological civilization.

God cannot take part in demonstrations. God cannot write books. Because of God we can do those things and are called at times to do them. Let us expect of God only the kinds of things that God does, while taking our part by responding to God's ever-renewed call.

Sometimes, we can increase what is possible for God. What God can call a person to do is determined by what that person inherits from the past. If we expand someone's knowledge, we enable God to call them to new acts that require that knowledge.

This works at other levels as well. For example, one evidence of God's universal presence in nature is that bodies work to heal themselves. Cells aim at their own health and the contribution that, as healthy cells, they make to the body. But cells are affected by their environments. This, of course, includes the physical environment; also, medicines may help cells participate in the healing of the body.

The psychological environment is important as well. This is taken account of as the placebo effect in the testing of the effectiveness of medicines. And the cells in a sick body are affected by the spirit of visitors. Prayers can concentrate these effects. And the total effect in all the cells allows God to offer greater possibilities to the cells. God is the great healer, but we can work with God in individual healing as in healing society.

Receptiveness and responsiveness to God's call always works for ecological civilization. There is no requirement that one think about this inclusive goal. But God has called some to think about the inclusive goal and offer that understanding to others. Perhaps those who understand the common goal can receive calls from God that are not possible for those whose imagination is more limited. Some of us are called to develop and share the common vision. Others are called to give a cup of cold water to a thirsty stranger. Others are called to tell a joke. Others are called to express their love in a sexual embrace. Others are called to strive even harder in a race. Let us respect and love one another and put our hope in God's weaving out of our small contributions a habitable planet, sensible ideas, and a humane society.

Ingram Content Group UK Ltd.
Milton Keynes UK
UKHW012021040423
419617UK00005B/498